PARZIVAL

An Introduction

Eileen Hutchins

TEMPLE LODGE

Temple Lodge Publishing
Hillside House, The Square
Forest Row RH18 5ES

www.templelodge.com

Third edition 2012

First published by Temple Lodge in 1979; reprinted 1987;
second edition 1992

A catalogue record for this book is available from the British Library

ISBN 978 1 906999 35 3

Cover by Andrew Morgan Design incorporating German illuminated
manuscript image

Typeset by DP Photosetting, Neath, West Glamorgan
Printed and bound by 4edge Ltd.

CONTENTS

iii

FOREWORD

This book is the mature fruit of a life devoted to study, teaching and sharing with others the treasures of art and wisdom implicit in those works of literature which are included amongst the foundation stones of our Western spiritual culture.

Eileen Hutchins was English by birth and education. After taking her degree at Somerville College, Oxford, she entered the teaching profession. However, it was not long before she discovered that the style of instruction as well as the content of her lessons, which naturally reflected her own academic training, appeared to weaken her pupils' creative faculties rather than enhance them. Out of the inevitable disappointment and discouragement this aroused, she resolved to abandon her activity as a teacher in favour of social work.

It was at this turning point in her life that the pedagogical ideas of Rudolf Steiner, the Austrian philosopher and educator, were brought to her attention. In these she found what she had instinctively been searching for, and before long she was able to apply them in her teaching work with marked satisfaction and success.

Many years of teaching activity followed, in which the arts—music, painting, craftwork, eurythmy—played a vital role, enhancing and supplementing all she strove to awaken in her students as knowledge, love and appreciation of literature as an indispensable part of the cultural–spiritual heritage of every human being.

Eileen Hutchins was one of the pioneers in establishing and developing Elmfield School at Stourbridge, where she was long an active member of the College of Teachers. In addition, she shared in holding teacher-training seminars in various centres, lectured widely in this country, and wrote numerous articles on education and related aspects of the work of Rudolf Steiner.

Those many students and others who had the joy of experiencing at first hand her memorable discussions of great works of literature will welcome this book by one whom they warmly appreciated as a teacher and friend.

On the other hand, it is a pleasure and privilege to introduce Eileen Hutchins to that wider circle of readers who now meet her for the first time through the pages of this book, which unfolds something of the artistic beauty and spiritual wisdom of one of the mightiest works of world literature and—even more important—shows clearly its relevance to some of the most urgent problems of our time and their ultimate solution.

Paul M. Allen
Vidaråsen Landsby
Andebu, Norway
February 1992

ACKNOWLEDGEMENTS

It is not possible to mention by name all who have contributed to this booklet either through the sharing of ideas or the raising of questions. But I am deeply grateful for the interest that has been evoked.

However my heartfelt thanks are especially due to Paul Allen for his patient help in reading through the manuscript and for his enlightening comments on many of the leading themes.

INTRODUCTION

This introduction to Wolfram von Eschenbach's *Parzival* is primarily intended for those who are not already well acquainted with the poem. It is designed for readers who have not yet come into contact with it or have met it only through Wagner's interpretation. There are relatively few in this country who know it well; yet it is the only medieval romance obtainable in English which gives a truly consistent account of the Grail story. English readers brought up on Malory's *Morte Darthur*, or Tennyson's *Idylls of the King*, are often unaware of the distinction between the Arthurian and the Grail knights, and the vision of the Grail is too readily accepted as a vague mystical experience attainable only by those who have renounced their full humanity.

Eschenbach's *Parzival* and Dante's *Divine Comedy* are the two great peaks of medieval poetry, but, whereas Dante offers a mighty vision from the standpoint of life after death, Eschenbach presents the striving of the human being to bring spiritual values into life on earth. He gives us a wide view of the turmoil of the Middle Ages both in its idealism and its barbarity. We are introduced to characters of all ages and ranks; there are knights who are devoted to a noble ideal, and tyrants who bring suffering and disorder; there are old men who have attained dignity and wisdom, and lively, innocent children in their first encounter with the world of chivalry. Eschenbach is outstanding among medieval poets in his reverence for love in the marriage relationship and in his appreciation of the part played by women. There are many examples of their faithfulness and devotion in times of sorrow and loss. He is also the first medieval poet to represent a character who has to win his way through trial and error, from ignorance to wisdom, and from fascination with the world of the senses to recognition of higher realms of experience. In this sense he is representative of modern man.

1

The Poet

Little is known about the poet beyond what he himself tells us. From allusions in the poem it is assumed that he was born about AD 1170 and that *Parzival* was completed early in the thirteenth century. His work portrays him as a knight and he seems to have taken more pride in his calling than in his gifts as a poet. He makes many humorous allusions to his poverty and he says in *Parzival* that he does not know a letter of the alphabet, which is sometimes taken to mean that he could neither read nor write. This is supported by the fact that he never says, 'I read' but always, 'as it was told me' or 'as I heard'. However, because of the elaborate construction of the poem, scholars doubt whether his statement should be taken seriously, and consider that he was probably mocking the more intellectual poets of his time who regarded him as ignorant.

From the poem we gain a powerful impression of his vitality and of his wide human sympathies. He lives in the adventures which he describes. His style is that of a narrator not of a writer. He draws his listeners in to share the excitement of the battles and the sorrows of those who suffer. His many humorous comments imply an intimate relationship with his audience.

Eschenbach claims that he learned the story of Parzival from Kyot, the Provençal, who had found the source of the legend written in 'heathen' writing in Toledo. Scholars have been unable to trace any corresponding historical character and we receive the impression that we are in the presence of a mystery. Rudolf Steiner (1861–1925), the Austrian philosopher and educator, speaks of Eschenbach as a great initiate, so we can assume that he was connected with the Mystery Centres from which flowed forth the Imaginations needed at certain turning points of time.

The poem appeared shortly before the tragic events which shattered the unity of the Roman Catholic Church and aroused distrust in the honour of princes. Rudolf Steiner has confirmed that the prototype of Eschenbach's hero actually lived between the eighth and ninth centuries after Christ, but the story of his life and the influence he imparted were known only to a small circle until Chrétien de Troyes and Eschenbach popularized the theme in their poems. While the events described have their historical

2

setting in the ninth century, the actual details of everyday life reflect the times in which Wolfram himself lived.

Rudolf Steiner spoke of the stories of the loss of Paradise and of Parzival as two of the mightiest Imaginations ever given to mankind; and on this account above all it would seem important for Eschenbach's poem to be brought to a wider public.

Note on the Different Translations

Not until the last century was *Parzival* translated into modern German and it has since appeared in several different versions.

In 1894 it was rendered into English in poetic form by Jessie Weston,[1] who dedicated her work to the memory of Richard Wagner. A very readable prose translation by Helen Mustard and Charles Passage[2] was produced in 1961.

As there exist over 70 more or less complete manuscripts from the Middle Ages, it is not surprising that there are some variations, and translators have made use of different versions. As Jessie Weston did not follow the same edition as that available to Helen Mustard and Charles Passage, there are some divergences. I have followed the story from the latter version as this is more readily obtainable by those who would like to go more deeply into the theme, but the spelling of the characters' names, particularly those of Arthur's court, in Jessie Weston's rendering is much closer to English traditions, and so in this matter I have consulted her.

THE HISTORICAL BACKGROUND

At the beginning of the present century legends and folk tales were scarcely taken seriously. By many they were regarded as stories suitable only for children, by others as fantasies that were demoralizing because they were thought to present what was untrue.

We have seen a great change since then. Partly through the influences of Jung's interpretation of myths and dreams, and partly through the sheer vitality of the legends themselves, they are now widely recognized as having their own realms of reality.

The epics of Homer, which in translation still continue to be best-sellers, present us with what Jung calls archetypes. Figures and situations appear which have a special meaning, for the poems tell of a turning point in time when hitherto undeveloped human faculties were beginning to emerge. Homer did not consider himself the originator of his stories, but felt that he was divinely inspired. The *Iliad* commences with the words: 'Tell, O goddess, of the wrath of Achilles'; and the *Odyssey* opens with the line: 'Sing, O Muse, of the wanderings of Odysseus'.

Two heroes appear before us, the young and godlike Achilles and the wily Odysseus. Achilles is still in communion with the supersensible world and can call upon his goddess mother for aid; but Odysseus acts out of his own intelligence. He is developing a capacity for the future, the power of independent thinking free from the guidance of priest-king or religious tradition. Achilles is the more heroic figure but he is not able to capture Troy. Odysseus wins the day by devising the cunning plan of the wooden horse. In the *Iliad* he appears in many respects unworthy of our admiration, but in the *Odyssey* he earns his herohood by remaining constant to his quest and taking responsibility for his followers.

What is presented in the myths later comes to expression in recorded history. At the time of Greek ascendancy, spiritual knowledge had to a great extent been lost. When the oracles were consulted the replies were vague and ambiguous and could be interpreted only through the active intelligence of the receiver. But interest in science was developing and the philosophers, especially Socrates, Plato and Aristotle, were active in teaching their pupils to train their powers of thought so that they could rediscover the spiritual wisdom of the ancients through direct knowledge. We owe to the Greeks the concepts on which our educational, political and scientific theories have been founded.

With the Germanic or Nordic people the situation was quite different. They were not prepared for the kind of thinking developed by the Greeks. The word derived from the Old English 'methinks', that is to say, 'it thinks in me', illustrates their experience of thoughts being given to them by the outer world. We can tell from such poems as the Anglo–Saxon *Riddles* that they felt themselves at one with the ever-changing appearances of nature and the formative forces at work in all phenomena. The founding of a civilization or the amassing of vast possessions would have limited their freedom of movement, for they were possessed with the urge to test their strength by daring the unknown.

The *Volsunga Saga* illustrates their attitude to life. During the centuries immediately before the coming of Christ it was realized that the leadership of the gods had come to an end and for the future it was the hero who had to guide the race. Sigurd is represented as one who has to stand alone in slaying the dragon, winning the enchanted gold and riding through the flames to awaken the sleeping Valkyrie, representative of his higher being. The greatest virtue of the Nordic hero was to defy fate and assert undaunted courage in allying himself with the creative powers of nature.

This characteristic is shown in their later history. Anyone viewing the Viking ships in the museum at Oslo cannot but be astounded that in such frail vessels they could brave the fierce currents round the north of Scotland and weather the storms of the Atlantic to find America. They were fierce and terrible and would never acknowledge defeat. When, for example, the warrior Ragnar Lodbrog was captured by his enemies and thrown into a snake pit, he shouted triumphant war songs until overcome by the poison. Our present Western civilization owes to our Nordic heritage the urge to be free and direct our own lives.

However, it is more difficult to recognize the influence of the Celtic culture on our present way of life. In the third and fourth centuries preceding Christianity, the Celts spread across Europe from the Danube basin to the Black Sea and westward through France into the British Isles. They were later driven back or conquered by the Romans and subsequently by the various Germanic tribes. There was very little understanding or sympathy between the invaders and the Celts and so what had been developed in Britain and Gaul went long unnoticed.

The Celtic legends which are most widely known in this country are the stories of Arthur, but most of these have come to us through medieval French romances and have been considerably diluted by story-tellers who no longer knew their real meaning. We can find traces of their original character in the tale of Kilhwch and Olwen as told in the *Mabinogion*,[3] and in the fourteenth-century English poem of *Gawain and the Green Knight*.[4] There are also fragments of a ballad of *Gawain and the Loathly Lady*. The events described in these stories took place in a land which was still wild and uncultivated with great forests and impenetrable swamps, the haunts of savage beasts and evil men. In these grim solitudes dark, magical powers held sway.

It can be imagined that in the original foundation of the Round Table, Arthur's ideal was to create on earth a community able to reflect the harmony of the stars. The King and Queen with their 12 knights represented the sun and moon in their relationship with the 12 signs of the zodiac. On earth there was everywhere chaos, but in the heavens a divine order was made manifest which they strove to reflect.

In his course of lectures *Cosmic Christianity*,[5] Rudolf Steiner speaks of the Arthurian cult as having lasted for many centuries. It was at its highest stage of development in the third century before Christ at the time when Alexander the Great was leading his expeditions to the East. Professor Rhys, referred to in Charles Squire's *Celtic Myth and Legend*, claimed that there must have been a pre-Christian Arthur whose many legends were later attached to the fifth-century Roman–British chief who drove back the Saxons and with whom most modern scholars concern themselves. The legendary conquests of Arthur cannot be related to any fifth-century hero, but can well be supported by events in the fourth and third centuries before Christ when the Celts were still widely spread over Europe and were even able to capture Rome.

In the stories which are less under medieval influence the outstanding characteristic of the Arthurian knight is selfless devotion to the order. None seeks personal glory. In the English poem, Gawain, Arthur's nephew and his favourite knight, is prepared to undertake the perilous adventure with the Green Knight for the honour of Arthur's court. In the tale from the *Mabinogion* all Arthur's knights take a share in performing the tasks demanded of Kilhwch. It is only within the French romances that competitive tournaments are held for individual glory.

There is another important theme which is Celtic in origin. This is concerned with the awakening of individual love. In pre-Christian times love was closely related to the blood bond of family and tribe. Marriage was in a way a profession, dependent on a suitable training in the traditions and customs of the class to which the married couple belonged. Hence a union between members of different races was generally condemned. The Greeks valued fidelity between husband and wife, as is illustrated in the story of Odysseus and Penelope, but romantic love was thought to be brought about by the influence of Até, the goddess of confusion. Hence the passion of Phaedra for Hippolytus was destructive and terrible.

But just as the power of thinking and the ability to direct the forces of the will were only gradually developed as individual capacities, so in human relationships the winning of freedom from the bonds of blood and tradition came about only step by step. Early representatives of this impulse appear to us in legend. It is from Ireland that we derive three of the most famous love stories of early times: Tristan and Isolde, Deirdre of the Sorrows and Diarmaid and Grainne. Although the theme of Tristan and Isolde[6] is not known in its original Irish form and appears only in troubadour versions, scholars are in agreement about its Celtic source.

It is a mistake to imagine that these tales are forerunners of the theme of the eternal triangle. The love of Tristan and Isolde, unlike that of Lancelot and Guinivere, is not represented as

7

'guilty'. The knights who report the lovers' relationship to Mark are described as 'the traitor knights', and when Mark finds Tristan and Isolde sleeping in their bower in the woods a naked sword lies between them—the sign that their love is an ideal and not a physical relationship.

Their connection has its origin in a blood feud. Tristan has slain Isolde's cousin, Morholt, and when the splinter of his sword is found buried in the dead man's skull she vows that if ever she finds the owner of the sword that has lost this fragment she will kill him. There is a dramatic moment when Tristan, who has destroyed the dragon that was oppressing Ireland, is brought unconscious to the Queen to be healed. The Princess Isolde sees his sword and recognizes that he is the one she has been seeking. She is about to take his life when he opens his eyes and smiles at her. She knows then that she cannot kill him, but her hate remains unchanged until they drink the magic potion. It should not be imagined that their love is brought about through an enchantment which compels them against their will, although some of the medieval romances seem to imply this. It needs to be seen as the counter-picture of Sigurd's draught of forgetfulness by which his memory of the Valkyrie maiden, the image of his higher being, is obliterated. With Tristan and Isolde it is a draught of recognition. Each suddenly glimpses the higher being of the other. Blood feud and racial hostility are overcome in this Paradisal experience.

The tragedy for those who become aware of this ideal relationship is the difficulty of sustaining it in the vexations and trivialities of everyday life. The troubadours could find no solution to this problem. Hence their cult advocated the worship of a chosen lady to inspire their deeds from afar. There should be no physical connection, for this could lead only to disillusionment. The only consummation for ideal love lay in death.

The struggle to find a connection between a higher love and the companionship necessary for earthly life led to a development of love stories in two directions. The troubadour ideal found its highest expression in the poetry of Dante where the one he had loved from afar became after her death his inspirer and guide through the realms of Paradise. On the other hand the concern with the question of how love could become free of the blood bond and racial conventions led the story-tellers to become fascinated by what was regarded as illicit love; and so we have the romances where the lovers are human, all too human, like Lancelot and Guinivere, and Troilus and Cressida.

Both the Greek and the Norse races were aware that a divine wisdom had been lost to mankind. The Greeks spoke of a Golden Age in the distant past, and the Norse story of the death of Baldur represents the loss of spiritual vision. But through the development of individual faculties each group experienced a strengthening of self-awareness, which prepared the way for our modern materialistic civilization. The Celts on the other hand retained clairvoyance for a much longer period. Today in the Highlands of Scotland and the remoter districts of Ireland there are still found remnants of the old gift, often referred to as second sight. Memories lingered on of the selfless devotion required in the Arthurian order, and so a restraining influence was at work to counteract the danger of exaggerated egoism in the other races.

We can realize that each group followed a somewhat one-sided development. Living in the modern age we are called upon to be self-reliant and to bring our different capacities into a harmonious relationship. The one who has developed only his thinking powers is felt to be lacking in certain human qualities. The person whose will impulses are not controlled by thought is regarded as uncivilized. Unfair advantage is taken of those who act purely out of generosity. The events of history brought it about that the different racial groups were driven to influence and interact upon one another to create the forces needed for the present time.

To those living under the protection of the Roman Empire in the fifth century after Christ, the inroads of the Goths and later of the Vikings seemed to threaten their whole way of life. Yet the very events which endangered the structure of civilization brought new vigour to the luxurious and decadent Roman establishment. The Nordic tribes began to settle and absorb with enthusiasm a culture which they soon learned to admire. A new impulse also came from another source.

The Irish, who had never been conquered by the Romans, had developed a religious life of their own and in the fifth and sixth post-Christian centuries this began to flow into Europe. The entry of Christ into earthly existence had brought a new standard of values, but for several centuries the inspiration of Christianity could work only as a hidden leaven. When in AD 324 it was accepted by Constantine as the state religion, the teaching of Christ gradually became formulated into a system of dogma. But the Irish Church remained free of this. Christianity had not come to Ireland through the missionaries from Rome but through the Druids' supersensible experience of the events in Palestine. This is described in Fiona Macleod's story of St Bride and is confirmed by Rudolf Steiner. It is also recorded in the Chronicles of Prosper of Aquitaine that a year before St Patrick arrived in Ireland Pope Celestine sent his legate Palladius to those of the Irish who believed in Christ. The religious colleges in Ireland became famous and, particularly during the most turbulent years, there was a constant stream of pupils from Europe who came to study there.

From the sixth century onwards the movement was reversed. Missionaries set out from Ireland and, travelling to the South of France and the foothills of the Pyrenees, and, following the Rhine into Switzerland, they established centres of study where peace and order reigned amid the general confusion. Thus we find these different streams flowing together in preparation for the modern age.

During the turmoil of this time, so often called the Dark Ages, two more alien influences were having their effect upon Western Europe. In the seventh and eighth centuries the Arabs, inspired by the fanatical zeal of Mahomet, spread across North Africa, settled in Sicily and in due course conquered the whole of Spain. Although Mahomet had not demanded of his followers a highly developed intellectual knowledge, the Abbasid caliphs of Baghdad began to encourage special branches of learning, the highest attainment of which was reached in the reign of Harun-al-Rashid who died in AD 809.

At Harun's brilliant court, literature, philosophy and art flourished, but the subjects most keenly pursued were the different aspects of science, particularly astronomy, mathematics, chemistry and medicine. Much of the teaching of Aristotle, which had been lost to the West, was preserved in Asia Minor.

Enthusiasm for the sciences spread rapidly and centres were established in Spain, Sicily and Southern Italy. The very conflict of religious ideas between Christian and Moslem stimulated the thinkers of the West, and the ardour of teachers and scholars in the early universities owed much to Arabic thought.

We need to realize that at the time of Charlemagne, who was crowned Emperor by the Pope in AD 800, very few of the warrior caste in Europe could either read or write. Book-learning was the monopoly of the Church and those who occupied positions as chancellors, recorders or secretaries were clerics. Hence the intellectual brilliance of the Moslems made a deep impression. On the other hand, Harun-al-Rashid had a great admiration for the achievements of Charlemagne and the two exchanged presents. At this time behind the bitter conflicts there was concealed a great longing for collaboration between East and West.

In the meanwhile during these centuries a more hidden stream had been quietly finding its way into Europe. In the third century after Christ in Asia Minor a religious leader had appeared who strove to unite the wisdom of the different ancient mysteries in the light of Christianity. Manes, who was born around AD 216, brought an esoteric Christian wisdom which was vastly different from the dogmatic teaching developed later by the Roman Church. He described the descent of the Sun Being into the darkness, so that matter became penetrated by spirit.

He taught that evil was to be overcome not by conflict but by transformation through love. Evil had not been created as evil but had come into being in the course of evolution through falling behind the normal progress of the good. Hence it worked disturbingly as an element of darkness. Manes' teaching was illustrated in a legend. As in the course of time there came a separation of the darkness from the light, there arose in the depths a dragon who began to overpower and destroy all who opposed him. Then the King of the Paradise of Light created man and sent him down into the darkness to fight the dragon. Primeval man was armed with five powers, with breath and wind, with light, with water and fire. But the dragon appeared to win the fight and devoured man. However man had recognized and loved the King of the Paradise of Light and this love filled him with radiance. Thus gradually the dragon became irradiated from within and was filled with a longing for the light. Gentleness overcame hatred and the dragon was redeemed.

It can be seen that this is an entirely different teaching from that

11

developed by the Roman Church which more and more as time went on laid emphasis on the punishment of sin and the necessity of forcing the disobedient into submission.

Manes travelled widely and won a considerable following. In 1907, manuscripts of his teaching were found in the Gobi desert, marked here and there with Chinese symbols, and in 1930 more extensive records were discovered in southern Egypt. Until this century it was very difficult to find out anything about him because all testimony had been systematically destroyed.

For many years Manes had been protected by King Shapur but after the latter's death his son, King Bahram, had him tortured and slain. He was put to death, not on account of his religious teaching, but because he had failed to heal the King's son, though the cause of his failure is not known. However, after Manes' death[7] every effort was made to bring him into complete disrepute.

Nevertheless his influence spread through South Europe and by way of the Balkans and North Italy to the Pyrenees. In this neighbourhood, where there had been Celtic settlements, it found fertile ground for new development in the teaching of the Cathars.[8] This movement was the hidden source of inspiration for the troubadours. Manes had taught that religion, science and art should be one. He introduced the illustration of texts and prayer books, the singing of chants and the art of icon painting. Among the troubadours poetry and music expressed in a disguised form tenets of the Cathar teaching. In their songs the theme of ideal love which could be consummated only in death was not necessarily concerned with human relationships; in some cases it expressed yearning for the divine and the rapture of sense-free spiritual experiences. The poetry of St Francis of Assisi and St John of the Cross is steeped in the language of courtly love.

From the melting-pot of these many cultures and racial tensions there emerged the most glorious period of the Middle Ages. Between the tenth and thirteenth centuries there appeared the great cathedrals, the first universities, the illuminated manuscripts, the most beautiful craftsmanship in gold, ivory and gems, and the poetry and romances of the troubadours and minnesingers.

There was little feeling for nationality during this period. The inhabitants of Western Europe regarded themselves as members of

Christendom and the Church cast its mantle over all realms of life. The priests were bound by their solemn vows of poverty, chastity and obedience; knights dedicated their swords to God and to their overlord; craftsmen were united by the rules of their guild to uphold the quality of their craft and their loyalty to one another. In this time of outstanding artistic achievement each sphere of life had its established frame and, although as in every other epoch there were plenty of selfish and violent characters, there was general acceptance of the authority of the Church and few dared defy the threat of excommunication.

In the stained glass windows of the Cathedral of Chartres[9] we see represented not only the prophets and the saints but the Emperor Charlemagne and his paladins, the craftsmen at their tasks and the toilers on the land. The signs of the zodiac are in evidence to show that heaven and earth were in harmony, for labour itself was a path of redemption from the sin of Adam.

Only too soon the fabric of this social order was to be torn asunder. Never again would Christendom be so united. Lovers of medieval art and literature may well feel sorrow at the passing of this era, but we have to remember that the individual human being could never have attained to freedom if it had remained.

A new state of consciousness was emerging during the thirteenth and fourteenth centuries. Not only were the impulses to exert independent thinking and give rein to self-will at work among men but, except in scattered groups, the spiritual radiance of the first centuries of Christianity was fading. Heads of Church and state all too often failed to uphold the dignity of their position and the authority of priest and king came under attack. Although many noble characters were brought to the fore in asserting their independence of unworthy leaders, standards of conduct were undermined and the opportunities for evil were greatly enhanced. An immense step forward was necessary before mankind in general could support the responsibility of self-determination. The attainment of wisdom in the life of thought, harmony in the realm of feeling, and self-discipline in act and deed were far to seek.

Among the different races in pre-Christian times there appeared in myth and legend a foreshadowing of what was later to come about in the course of history. The question now arises whether any such archetypal picture was given as an example for our own epoch. Is there a legend where the central character can be said to illustrate the path of development needed by a modern human being? The answer can be found in the story of Parzival as related by Wolfram von Eschenbach.

THE POEM OF PARZIVAL

Book 1: Gamuret

The poet begins his theme with a strange comparison. We are told that a dauntless man's spirit is both black and white like the magpie's plumage. Both colours have a share in him, the colour of heaven and the colour of hell. Inconstancy is black like hell, while steadfast thoughts draw near to the brightness of heaven; and yet the one who strives may win his way to blessedness after all. It is here made clear that the leading theme of the poem is the struggle of the human being to transform his lower nature. The hero of the story is a brave man yet 'slowly wise', for the overcoming of darkness and the emergence into light is a long process and can be achieved only through steadfast endeavour.

The story is first of all concerned with Parzival's father, Gamuret of Anjou. As the younger son of a knight, he inherited nothing under Roman law from his father, and so set out for the East to win renown under the Baruch of Baghdad, who was said to have power over two thirds of the earth. This confirms the setting of the romance in the ninth century when leading figures in the West felt a great longing to contact the brilliant culture of the East. The mutual attraction between East and West is illustrated in history by the gifts exchanged between Harun-al-Rashid and Charlemagne. The Crusades were not launched until nearly three centuries later.

In the Baruch's service Gamuret changed his coat of arms from his family escutcheon of a panther to the sign of an anchor, for he felt the need of establishing himself in life. It is said that he won fame throughout heathendom and was admired by both Moslems and Christians.

In the course of his adventures he came to Zazamanc, a country of the Moors, where he was drawn into a remarkable conflict. The

Queen of the realm had been wooed by a Moorish Prince Isenhart, but she had refused to accept his love until he had proved his devotion in deeds of daring. In fighting to win her regard he lost his life. To avenge their lord his followers attacked Queen Belakane in her capital city of Patelamunt. At the same time a Christian army led by a Scottish noble, a vassal of Isenhart, joined the combat against the Queen.

We are told that there were 16 gates to Patelamunt, which during the war were never closed. Attacking the eight gates on the west was the dark-skinned Moslem army; against the eight gates on the east the Christians were assembled. The poem itself is divided into 16 books and in Wolfram's romance this number is also not without significance. Walter Johannes Stein, in his book on the ninth century,[10] points to the underlying meaning of this description. He regards the conquest of the city as the sign of a stage of inner development. In *Knowledge of the Higher Worlds*,[11] Rudolf Steiner writes of the Buddha's teaching of the eightfold path, the pursuit of which leads to the acquiring of spiritual capacities. He there describes how in ancient times man had instinctively, in a dulled state of consciousness, corresponding qualities which today are no longer active. By developing the faculties as taught by the Buddha the meditant can reawaken consciously the former powers.

In the conflict around Patelamunt the pre-Christian state of consciousness is represented by Isenhart, who met his death because the primordial faculties were no longer effective. His dark-skinned followers were fighting at the eight western gates facing the sunset, while the Christian knights in the eastern light of dawn were striving to acquire the new knowledge. However, they were not advanced enough to achieve their aim. Gamuret came and, by conquering both armies and being accepted as the Queen's husband, was able to restore peace. His victory enabled him to take over the splendid equipment of Isenhart: a magnificent tent, a helmet of diamond, a suit of armour and a sword. We may perhaps consider the tent as a sign of Gamuret's attainment of a particular degree of development, while the helmet, the suit of armour and the sword are the protectors of his three soul forces— his thinking, his feeling and his willing. These had served the pre-Christian hero Isenhart for a time, but he laid them aside to prove

16

his love for Belakane. His ancient instinctive powers could no longer protect him.

The conflict in which one army is black and the other white recalls the opening lines of the poem. The dark warriors are those trusting to an atavistic knowledge which has to be transformed; the white are those striving towards the light.

The teaching of the Buddha stemmed from the East but had its roots in a more ancient wisdom than Christian or Moslem had yet achieved. In his position as King of Patelamunt, Gamuret brought the leaders of both armies before the Queen to give her the kiss of peace. He was able to unite West and East but he had not acquired steadfastness. After a short while he became restless and, just before the birth of their son, he left Belakane in quest of further adventure. As the father was white and the mother black, the child was born streaked black and white. 'Like the magpie was the colour of his hair and skin'.

Thus we can see how the episodes in Book I illustrate the opening theme of the poem, the progress from darkness to light and the transforming of atavistic powers by means of clear consciousness.

Book 2: Herzeleide

On his return to France Gamuret learned of a grand tournament. Herzeleide, Queen of the realms of Norgals and Waleis, had arranged a contest in which the winner would be accepted as her husband and would share her rule. Without considering the obligations involved, Gamuret determined to try his strength against the many famous champions entering the lists. The poet gives an eloquent description of the splendour of Gamuret's approach, preceded by trumpeters, fiddlers and drummers, and of the setting up of the royal tent of Isenhart.

In the contest Gamuret overcame all opponents but his triumph brought him into difficulties. The King of France had just died and the widowed Queen Anflise now sent messengers to claim Gamuret as her rightful husband, because, in the course of his knightly training, he had chosen her as his ideal. On the other hand the rules of the tournament required that he should accept Queen Herzeleide. Gamuret stoutly refused both on the ground that he had a beloved wife in the East; but he found himself overborne. No one in a Christian country would acknowledge the validity of a pagan marriage. Finally Gamuret had to accept the ruling of the judges of the tournament. He sent a message to the Queen of France that he was still loyal to her as his ideal, but that this did not involve marriage, and he took Herzeleide as his wife. She won his love but again he could not settle. When he had first set out on his adventures he had prayed: 'My God show me the ways of blessedness.' He still felt that his quest was not yet fulfilled.

At the very moment of his victory in the tournament, Gamuret had received the sad news of his elder brother's death, on account of which he now became the ruler of Anjou. He reverted to the family crest of the panther, a sure sign that in his life of adventure he had not found a source of inner stability.

Some months after Gamuret's departure, Herzeleide lay one noontide in a restless slumber. Suddenly it seemed that lightning was flashing round her and she was caught up into the clouds. Thunder rolled, sparks of fire seemed to spring from her windblown hair and there came a violent rush of rain like burning tears. Then the dream changed. She had given birth to a dragon and was suckling it, but it sprang away from her and disappeared never to return. She awoke in anguish to find that a messenger had arrived with tragic news. Her husband had lost his life fighting in the East. His death had been brought about by treachery. Resting from combat in the noonday heat, Gamuret had removed his armour and the diamond helmet he had won from Isenhart. An envious knight, through the spells of black magic, softened the diamond that had hitherto withstood the hardest steel. When Gamuret awoke to the cry of battle and rushed into the conflict, his enemy's sword pierced through the helmet and Gamuret met his death.

The Baruch ordered a costly funeral. An epitaph, engraved on the diamond helmet and secured above his grave, proclaimed his many triumphs and included the words: 'He was baptized in the Christian faith, yet his death was a grief to Saracens.

'Wish him bliss who lies here.'

18

Gamuret had the courage and qualities of heart to unite West and East, but he lacked constancy and so the forces of evil were able to overcome him. The task in which he had failed would devolve upon his son Parzival.

Herzeleide for a while gave way to violent grief, but she was already bearing Gamuret's child and she summoned up her strength for the sake of their son. A fortnight later she gave birth to a sturdy boy and comforted herself fondling him and calling him by the endearing terms of 'Bon fils, cher fils, beau fils'. However, she was determined that on no account should he follow in the steps of his father, so leaving their three kingdoms in the charge of a regent she took him away into the woods of Soltane and brought him up as a child of nature, entirely removed from all contact with the culture of his time. She ordered her servants never to mention knighthood or speak to him of the life he was being denied.

Book 3: Gurnemanz

We find in many legends that the hero who is to bring a new impulse to mankind needs in early life to be protected from the customs and traditions of his time. It was well for Parzival that he was saved from the elaborate and artificial codes of medieval chivalry. He grew up with all the wonder and unrepressed delight of childhood. In his woodland home there were no luxuries; he washed in the stream, he made his own bow and arrows and helped the servants hunt for food. He knew nothing of death, and when he shot down the birds and silenced their singing he wept.

There was one lesson his mother taught him which brings to mind the leading theme of the poem. When he asked her, 'What is God?' she replied, 'He is brighter than the daylight, yet He took upon Himself the features of man. Pray to Him when in trouble for His fidelity has ever offered help to the world. But there is one called the Master of Hell, and he is black and faithlessness is his mark. From him turn your thought away, and also from inconstant wavering.'

One day when Parzival was roaming through the woods, four members of King Arthur's court came riding past to rescue a maiden whom two knights were carrying away by force. The leader, who was in shining armour, asked Parzival if the fugitives had passed that way. The boy knelt in reverence for he imagined that this shining figure must be God. When the leader told him about Arthur's court and the noble order of knighthood, Parzival questioned them in wonder about their armour and their weapons. They were astonished that this beautiful lad could be so ignorant and, finding that he could give them no help, they rode on their way.

The boy went at once to his mother and told her about the riders who were 'more shining than God'. He demanded a horse so that he could ride away at once to become a knight at Arthur's court. Herzeleide was grieved to the heart; she dressed him in the garb of a fool and mounted him on a poor knock-kneed pony that stumbled at every step, for she thought that when folk mocked him he would be glad to come back to her. But so great was her sorrow that as he rode away she fell lifeless to the ground.

All unconscious that he had caused his mother's death, Parzival went on his way until he came to a lordly pavilion. Its owner, Prince Orilus, had ridden out, leaving his wife Jeschuté resting. Parzival made his way into the tent. Herzeleide had given him misleading advice about how to greet ladies; she said he should kiss them and ask for a token, perhaps a ring. He saw Jeschuté sleeping so he went to kiss her and snatched her ring and brooch; then he helped himself to the food and drink laid out on a table. Jeschuté was alarmed but felt she could do nothing against someone so strong. She could only beg him to leave her. Soon after he had gone, Orilus returned. When Jeschuté told her tale he was convinced that she had encouraged the lad, and, in his jealous rage, he tore off her rich clothing, leaving her only a linen smock, and, mounting her on a miserable nag, led her through the countryside to shame her as an example of a faithless wife.

Parzival was riding on his way, blissfully ignorant of the wrong he had done, when he came upon a maiden, holding a dead knight in her arms. She was weeping and tearing her long brown braids for grief. The simple boy addressed her with mingled pity and curiosity. He was anxious to know whether the knight were dead and who had done this deed. In spite of her grief the maiden perceived the boy's true nature. She greeted him with the words,

'You have virtue in you. Honour be to your sweet youth and to your lovely face. In truth you will be rich in blessings.'

When she asked his name, all he knew was that his mother had called him, 'Bon fils, cher fils'. She at once recognized him, for she was his cousin Siguné, who long ago had been cared for by his mother. From her for the first time Parzival learned his name. She also told him that Schionatulander, the dead knight for whom she mourned, had lost his life at the hand of Orilus while defending Parzival's domains. He had died for Parzival's sake. The lad was at once eager to avenge her lover's death, but she misdirected him, fearing that he could be no match for a seasoned warrior. Parzival was to meet Siguné twice again in the course of his wanderings and each time he was to gain self-knowledge.

At last he reached Arthur's court which had just been shaken by an act of revolt. Ither of Gaheviess, known as the Red Knight, was indignant that Arthur had given a judgment against him. To express his contempt he had ridden into the hall, snatched a golden goblet from the table, spilling the wine over the Queen's lap, and had defied any knight who dared to come and claim it from him in combat. As the leading knights were absent on adventure, no one responded. Parzival's arrival in quest of knighthood aroused merriment among the squires and pages, but when he heard that no one was willing to challenge the Red Knight he demanded the task. Against his better judgement, Arthur was persuaded to agree.

Among the courtiers was a maiden, Kunnewaaré, who was doomed never to laugh until she beheld the one who was to win supreme honour. In his fool's dress, Parzival rode out, and she laughed but in joy not mockery. Sir Kay, indignant that she was laughing at such an unworthy object, struck her severely. This made a deep impression on Parzival; again someone had innocently suffered on his behalf.

On the meadow outside the town the Red Knight was waiting for combat. When a lad in fool's garment, riding on a shabby horse, challenged him, he could not take it seriously, and with the butt end of his spear pushed Parzival off his mount. Leaping to his feet in anger, Parzival flung a javelin, aiming at the eye slot in the Red Knight's armour. The aim was true; the weapon, entering the eye, pierced the brain and the Red Knight fell dead.

It was an age of bloodshed when many knights lost their lives in

21

such encounters; and Parzival felt no compunction for his deed. The Red Knight's horse and armour were his by right of conquest, but he had no idea how to unarm the dead man. Fortunately for him a young squire, Iwanet, had followed at a distance to see the outcome. He now came foward and helped arm Parzival and mount him on the Red Knight's horse. Aware of the mockery he had met at Arthur's court, Parzival realized he must earn his place in knightly society before returning, but he asked Iwanet to report his victory and express his sorrow to the Lady Kunnewaaré.

Parzival set off and, galloping in one day a distance that any unarmed sensible man would do in two, he arrived at the castle of the old knight Gurnemanz. There was astonishment when his armour was removed and a lad in fool's raiment was disclosed. But Gurnemanz realized his quality and took him in hand to teach him knightly conduct and courtly manners. There was one item of Gurnemanz's teaching which was to play an important part in Parzival's later progress. He was taught not to ask questions, for what he was ripe to receive would be revealed in due course. This was the customary method of education of the time. There exist Latin books from the Middle Ages which give a series of questions and answers which the pupils had to learn by heart. A last survival today is in the catechism of the Anglican Church.

When his guest had acquired what was necessary, Gurnemanz suggested that, as his own sons had been killed in combat, Parzival should marry his daughter Liasse and become his heir. This would have given Parzival an established position and he was already romantically attracted by the lovely girl, but he felt that he had not yet found his rightful place in life. He was not at this stage fit for such a position, so, saying farewell, he set out once more.

Book 4: Kondwiramur

Parzival had now attained a certain stage of development and this is indicated in a very brief episode described in only a few lines of the poem. We are told that he came to a swinging bridge of wickerwork spanning a wild torrent. It had no rope or handrail and his horse refused to cross. One incautious step either to left or right would have landed them in the tumultuous waters below. Parzival dismounted and led his horse across the abyss without mishap.

We can compare this incident with the adventure of Odysseus when he had to pass between Scylla and Charybdis. This expresses in an imaginative form the quality of balance and the ability to avoid extremes. Parzival had attained the power of judgement and so in his next adventure he was able to make the right decision.

By nightfall he came to the beleaguered city of Pelrupar, but, as fighting for that day was over, he succeeded in winning an entry. He was greeted by the inhabitants with courtesy, his armour was removed, and water was brought from the well for him to wash away the iron rust. In return he offered them his service if they were in need. A message was sent to the Queen Kondwiramur who, accompanied by her two uncles, the Dukes Kiot and Manfilot, came to welcome him.

Owing to the siege all were weak from lack of food, but Kiot and Manfilot owned a hunting lodge in a wild mountain glen and were able to bring a supply of provisions. At Parzival's suggestion they shared these out among the starving townsfolk so that there was little left for Kondwiramur and her guest, but they shared it in harmony. Remembering Gurnemanz's teaching, Parzival was silent in her company, but, realizing that it was the duty of the hostess to make the first move, she thanked him for his offer of service. He learned that she was the niece of Gurnemanz, whose son Schenteflur had died fighting on her behalf.

After their meagre supper Parzival was conducted to his bed. The events of the night are told in such a way that they can be interpreted as a visionary experience. Around Parzival's bed the candlelight was as bright as day, when the Queen in her nightgown of white silk slipped softly without a sound into his chamber and knelt weeping before him. He took her into his bed. There was no passionate love, but he became aware of her deep distress. King Klamidé, by besieging her city, was trying to force her to marry him, but she had decided to throw herself into the moat rather than yield. Moved by her beauty and her sorrow, Parzival resolved to defend her. Then she glided away and no one was so wise that he perceived her going.

According to the custom of the times, if a knight championed a lady attacked by an unwelcome wooer, he himself was committed to marrying her. Parzival felt sorrowful at the thought of renouncing Liasse but he realized that his rightful task was to support the Queen and he resolved to confront Klamidé.

When he had successfully overthrown the enemy, he sent him to report at Arthur's court and surrender to the maiden Kunnewaaré in recompense for the insult she had suffered on Parzival's account when he had first appeared there in fool's garb.

Parzival had now won a kingdom and a bride. We are told that he felt such reverence for his wife that it seemed to him unfitting to approach her passionately and the marriage was not consummated until the third night. They loved each other with true and lasting affection. The kingdom was soon restored to order, ships arrived with provisions and Parzival saw to the fair distribution of supplies.

For a while all was joy, but soon Parzival asked his wife if he might leave her for a short time to find out how his mother was faring, for he had received no news of her since he had left the woods of Soltane. Little did he know that the time of his absence from Kondwiramur would be long and sad.

Until now we can picture Parzival's adventures as taking place in the physical world. Although many of them represent deeper experiences than the outer events might imply, the story has nevertheless followed his progress in learning to find his way in the world and the poet's descriptions give a vivid picture of the life of the times. Parzival had overcome the impetuous exuberance of youth and had acquired the ability to act out of a sound judgement. This phase of his development the Greeks would have well understood. But from now on the story enters another realm.

Book 5: Anfortas

The poet begins the fifth book with the warning that much suffering lies in store for the son of Gamuret; however, there will also be a reward. He will later achieve joy and great honour.

Parzival set out in quest of his mother, who had already passed through the portal of death. His subsequent adventure was also closely connected with another figure who had died on his account, the young Schionatulander. We are told that as he rode he was so troubled by thoughts of his beautiful young wife that he allowed his horse to take what path it pleased, and so, without a conscious aim, he rode further in that one day than a bird with ease could have flown. He met no human being and passed no sign of a dwelling.

In the evening he came to a mountain lake where from a barge, anchored near the shore, a number of men were fishing. Among them was a kingly-looking figure who wore a hat adorned with peacock feathers. Parzival asked him if there was any place near at hand where he could spend the night. The fisherman replied that there was nowhere within 30 miles unless he rode straight on. He would then reach a castle in which the fisherman himself would later be his host. But he warned Parzival to be careful for there were many roads that led no one knew where and it was easy to miss the way.

At the top of the hill Parzival saw the castle with its many turrets and marvellous fortifications. He thought that no besieging army could ever seize such a fortress, for an abyss lay between him and the protecting walls. In reply to his call that the fisherman had sent him, the drawbridge was lowered. Parzival was kindly received and the squires who tended him did not let him observe how sorrowful was the mood of all within. They removed his armour and brought him a beautiful cloak of Arabian silk loaned him by the Queen. When he had washed the rust from his hands and face, it seemed to them all as though a new day had dawned.

Parzival was led to the great hall for their evening meal. A hundred chandeliers gave light, a hundred couches, each seating four knights, were arranged through the hall, and on three great fireplaces logs of sweet-smelling wood were burning. Parzival saw his host on a couch near the central fire. He was obviously suffering and, in spite of the heat of the fire, was wrapped in splendid furs of black and grey sable. But he welcomed his guest warmly and asked him to sit beside him.

Suddenly the door opened and a squire dashed in, carrying a lance dripping with blood. At his entry all present sank to their knees, weeping and groaning, until he had circled the hall and departed. Then the mourning ceased.

After this there came a strange ritual procession. Twenty-four maidens, their hair decked with flowers, entered the hall in groups. The first four were dressed in brown, two bore candles and two carried ivory trestles. They were followed by eight in robes greener than grass, four bearing lights and four a table-top carved from a single jewel. Four more who carried lights were accompanied by two with sharp silver knives. The last group, wearing coloured silks interwoven with gold, had vessels of clear glass in which sweet-smelling balsam was burning. After them came the Queen Repanse de Schoie at whose entry it seemed that the sun was rising. The poet describes how she bore 'that thing which is called the Grail'. This was placed before the host and from it each knight procured whatsoever nourishment he most desired, both of food and drink.

Parzival gazed in wonder and longed to question the meaning of what he saw, but he remembered the teaching of Gurnemanz and remained silent. Presently his host summoned a squire to bring a sword, encased in a jewelled sheath and with a hilt of a single ruby. He presented it to Parzival with the words, 'Since God wounded me, you are the one fitted to wear this sword. You will find it a sure defence.' Once more Parzival longed to question his host but was again restrained by the counsel of Gurnemanz.

The feast came to an end and the Grail procession withdrew. As the Grail bearer passed out of the door, Parzival caught a glimpse into an antechamber. There lay the most beautiful old man that he had ever beheld; he was greyer than the morning mist. It was Titurel to whom the angels had entrusted the guardianship of the Grail.

The host now sadly suggested that Parzival should retire as he must be weary from his long journey. The visitor was conducted with all ceremony to his rest and soon fell asleep. But that night he was tormented with dreams which caused him as much anguish as that suffered by Herzeleide when she felt she had given birth to a dragon and woke to hear of her husband's death. All night long Parzival imagined that he was in the rush of battle, thrust at with countless spears and overthrown by a charge of horses. He felt that his pain was a presage of sorrow to come.

When at last he woke to full consciousness the morning was well advanced. No squires came to call him but he saw his clothes and armour laid out ready for him. He dressed hurriedly and went through the corridors, calling and searching for his companions of the evening before, but no one was to be found. In the courtyard his steed stood saddled and waiting. The ground was trampled and the drawbridge down as though the whole company had ridden out. Parzival mounted and rode hastily after them. He was sure now that he must find out the meaning of what he had experienced. As he was crossing the drawbridge, before he had reached the other side, it was drawn up so suddenly that his horse was flung onto the opposite bank and Parzival nearly lost his seat. He heard the words shouted after him: 'Ride on and bear the hatred of the sun. You are a goose.'

Parzival did not understand the meaning of these words, but he felt that in some way he had failed. He imagined that his host and followers were engaged in combat and needed his help, so it was important for him to find them as soon as possible. For a while he could follow their tracks, but soon all traces were lost and he no longer knew the way.

At this moment he heard the sound of weeping and he came upon a woman sitting in a linden tree, holding in her arms the dead and embalmed body of a knight. She had become so wasted and pale that Parzival did not at first recognize her as his cousin Siguné, but he expressed his grief at her distress. She was surprised that anyone could venture unharmed into this wild region where many had lost their lives, and she warned him to turn back. When Parzival told her he had spent the night at the castle, she thought he was deceiving her, for no one could enter there unless it revealed itself to the seeker. When he affirmed that he had seen many wonders, she recognized him and saw that he was wearing the sword given him by Anfortas. She told him of its strange powers. It bore upon its blade mystic signs. It would serve him well at the first stroke, but at the second it would break, and the owner would have to reweld it by dipping it before dawn in a magic spring.

As the sword revealed to her that Parzival must truly have been at the castle, she assumed that he had asked the question which would bring release to the suffering King. It had been foretold to the servers of the Grail that, when a young and innocent knight found his way to them and asked the suffering King what ailed him, Anfortas would be freed from his pain and the newcomer

27

would take his place. From this account it is clear that Siguné was connected with the Grail circle.

When she found that Parzival had failed, she accused him of being accursed and of having the fangs of a venomous wolf. Parzival begged for a kindlier word before they parted but she remained adamant, declaring that he had lost his honour, and Parzival parted from her with a sense of deep remorse. Through this second meeting with Siguné he had again advanced a step in self-knowledge. In spite of his success in winning himself a kingdom and a beautiful wife, he had failed in this more demanding enterprise.

What Parzival had seen and felt can perhaps be understood in the light of our sleep experiences. Until recently most people who were healthy and well balanced took it for granted that, after going to sleep tired out, they would wake up the next morning restored and ready to face the new day. But they rarely asked what happened during the night to renew their strength. A study of dreams has shown that during this period of darkened conscious-ness we are working over and elaborating what has happened during the day, and are converting our experiences into fantastic pictures. Most people suffer at times from anxiety dreams in which the worries of everyday life assume bewildering forms, or certain premonitions appear in warning. But some dreams are more uplifting. Dreamers can become aware of fountains of sparkling water or of mountain breezes, more refreshing than anything known in the waking state, and they rise in the morning filled with new hope and vigour. Sometimes the course of their own life appears to them in a symbolic picture; for instance, after passing through deep waters and a dark cave, they emerge into glorious sunlight, or, after struggling through dense mist up a mountain slope, they meet the dawn.

Rudolf Steiner has shown that, when in sleep we are freed from the domination of our sense experiences, certain innate powers are liberated to create our dream pictures. In passing over into dreamless sleep we are entering the realm from which we came at birth. We are once more united with the creative powers of the divine world. We bring back refreshing forces, but in general we are unconscious of what we have received. However, if it were not for this nightly experience, our physical bodies would disintegrate.

28

As he was searching for his dead mother, Parzival had become to a certain degree free from his absorption in the sense world, so that he was able to perceive his experiences in the realm of sleep in the form of imaginative pictures, but he could not rise to an understanding of what they represented. Only after much suffering would he be able to attain a fully conscious knowledge.

On the physical plane it would seem that Parzival had come into contact with a community united with a stream of esoteric Christianity which could be understood only by those who were in some way specially prepared. Hence the Grail Castle is described as invisible except for those to whom it reveals itself. Their leader had been unfaithful to his calling and so the community had suffered a decline. We learn later of his having deserted the service of the Grail in quest of love adventures. This betrayal brought him intense suffering, the chief effect of which was to render him powerless to fulfil his task. Parzival was the one who would eventually renew the cult but he was not yet sufficiently mature. The account of what happened in the Grail Castle gives a series of Parzival's Imaginations, which express supersensible realities in picture form.

Every detail needs to be taken seriously. The castle was in a wild and dangerous realm, separated from the surrounding country by an abyss. On entering it, Parzival had to take off his armour and wear the rich silk robe lent him by the Queen; that is to say, he was now called upon to develop a different state of consciousness from that required in his everyday life. The knights of this order were guardians of the life-giving and healing forces of Christianity. We can thus understand how the Grail gave to each one who partook the nourishment which he especially required. The ritual procession of the Grail can remind us of the creative forces of the plant world. The maidens of the first group, who bore the supporting trestles, were clad in brown; those who followed, carrying the table-top and the silver knives, were in green brighter than grass; the last group, with lamps burning scented oil, were in coloured silks threaded with gold. In the plant world we see substance repeatedly transformed. The 24 maidens can be regarded as reflections of high spiritual powers at work in this transformation. The nourishment given by the Grail was not physical but spiritual; the cult as it is described here is an imaginative picture which includes elements of the traditional Christian Mysteries of transubstantiation and of the communion service.

We now need to consider the other events, the squire carrying the bleeding lance and the gift of the sword. An important experience in the realm of dreams is our relationship with other human beings. What happens in everyday life can in a dream appear in an entirely different light. In the daytime we may have a serious clash with a close friend, but in the night we can come to realize that our disagreement is trivial and irrelevant in view of our true connection with each other. On the other hand we can be charmed and led into committing ourselves with a stranger and, in a dream, experience a dark shadow.

Parzival had received an impression of Anfortas's inner being. The bleeding lance can be regarded as an image of the King's misdirected will life which had brought such sorrow to the community, while the sword is an indication of a faculty which he had forfeited through his failure as Grail King. Hence he passed the sword on to Parzival as his hoped-for successor. Siguné explained that this sword could be used only once; at the second stroke it would break and have to be rewelded before it could be used again. The human being possesses a faculty which can be used only once in the same way. This we commonly speak of as Inspiration. There comes a sudden flash of perception which does not depend on logical reasoning but which can give the clue to an understanding of a person or situation so that the right relationships can be brought about. As the circumstances can never be exactly the same again, this particular Inspiration can never be repeated. The capacity itself has to be reawakened. As Inspirations spring from the feeling life, it is said the sword had to be dipped in the magic well before sunrise, that is to say, before the hour of full waking-day consciousness.

After his parting with Siguné, Parzival's life entered a new phase. He began to compensate for his early mistakes. He met with Orilus displaying Jeschuté to the world as an unfaithful wife. To prove Jeschuté's innocence Parzival attacked the Prince and found himself engaged in a fierce combat. Orilus bore on his shield the sign of a dragon and above his helmet a second reared its head; countless more were embroidered on his surcoat so that Parzival felt himself engaged with a hundred dragons, representative of

Orilus's passionate nature. However, he himself was fired by the ideal of justifying the one who had suffered through his folly, and in his strength he was victor. By returning Jeschuté's ring and vowing her innocence on the holy relics of the hermit Trevrezent, he made the Prince accept his wife once more into favour. Then he sent him to do homage to King Arthur and submit to Kunnewaaré who was in fact Orilus's sister. When at last he reached Arthur's court, Orilus recognized his sister's tent by the sign of the dragon displayed above it. It stood just above the source of a spring which Rudolf Steiner refers to as the well of Inspiration where the Grail sword could be rewelded, and which was guarded by Kunnewaaré.

Book 6: Arthur

Parzival continued in his quest for the Grail. Although it was late spring, the time of Pentecost, there was a fall of snow, and as he passed through a dark forest he came to a spot where a wild goose, wounded by a falcon, had shed three drops of blood. Parzival was transfixed at the sight. The white snow, the red blood and the dark trees called to mind the white skin, the red lips and the dark hair of his wife Kondwiramur, and he was overcome with longing. The outer events of the story now reflect Parzival's inner condition.

The words, 'Bear the hatred of the sun. You are a goose,' had sounded after him as he left the Grail Castle. Lost on his way, oppressed by his failure, he was himself like the wounded goose. One of the Templar Knights' symbols was the swan of which he had proved himself unworthy. Gazing at the blood drops, he fell into a trance.

All unaware, Parzival was now in the neighbourhood of Arthur's court and the news was brought by Kunnewaaré's squire that a strange knight was near at hand as though in preparation for battle. An ambitious young knight, Segramor, won permission to go and challenge the intruder. Lost in his trance, Parzival made no response, but, when attacked, he suddenly became conscious and struck Segramor from his horse. Then he was once more caught in the spell of his love and longing. Segramor returned to Arthur's court discomforted and Sir Kay rode out, only to suffer a harsher fate. In the attack, his horse was killed and he himself fell, breaking his right arm and his left leg. In this way Kay received punishment for his treatment of Kunnewaaré. Only when Gawain appeared was Parzival freed from his spell.

In most of the legends concerning him, Gawain appears as a character of sympathy and insight. He immediately realized Parzival's condition and, taking a silk scarf, he laid it over the blood drops and wakened Parzival from his trance. By now all at Arthur's court knew of the exploits of the slayer of Ither of Gaheviess, whom they called the Red Knight, as they were ignorant of his true name. Gawain offered to serve Parzival and to conduct him to the King.

From now on an intimate connection is indicated between Gawain and Parzival, and on this account the following adventures of Gawain are of importance, although some readers regard them as an interlude. It was Gawain who released Parzival from his trance and prepared the way for his further progress. Parzival had not been able to free himself from longing and desire. He had been caught in the realm of his Imaginations. Although he possessed the sword of Inspiration, he had not yet attained the maturity to use it. Now through Gawain's help he could renounce picture imagery and live in the feeling life of others without losing his own identity.

Parzival was welcomed into Arthur's order with joy, especially by Kunnewaaré to whom he had shown such homage. However, he could never have achieved the task to which he was called if he had remained there. The Arthurian cult was in its decline. In many legends of the thirteenth century Arthur is represented as losing his power of leadership, and in this story he is an onlooker but not a performer. When Parzival first appeared at his court and demanded the contest with the Red Knight, it was Kay who urged Arthur to agree. Later the King wished to refuse Segramor the right to challenge Parzival, but Guinevere, wishing to give Segramor his chance, persuaded her husband to change his mind. While Parzival was now glad to be accepted into the Arthurian community, destiny denied him such a retreat.

Just as Parzival had given his pledge to the knightly fellowship, there rode into the circle a strange intruder. She was hideous to look upon for she had black hair as coarse as that of a pig, and black eyebrows so long they had to be gathered into plaits. Her nose was like a dog's and her skin rough and hairy; she had two horrible tusks and claws like a lion. Yet this alarmingly ugly woman wore rich apparel and peacock feathers in her hat, for she was Kondrie, the messenger of the Grail.

She denounced Arthur for harbouring one who would bring him into disrepute. She then turned to Parzival and cursed him. He had failed in honour, he had received a sword of which he was unworthy and he had been false to the Grail King. His treachery was like the adder's fang. Not only did she make Parzival aware that he had lacked compassion for Anfortas, she also implied that his half-brother Feirefis stood in greater honour than he. A visiting queen from the East was able to tell Parzival more about his brother. He was a rich and generous ruler, worshipped like a god, and his skin had the sheen of a magpie's feathers, streaked black and white.

The figure of Kondrie presents a mystery. She is a messenger of the Grail and yet she appears to Parzival in a terrifying form. Often in life a blow of fate which seems most shattering drives the recipient into the position for which he is best fitted. Parzival could never have fulfilled his destiny if he had remained at Arthur's court.

Before she left, Kondrie made mention of another castle strangely related to that of the Grail. She asked if there was no noble knight prepared to win fame by seeking the four queens and the four hundred maidens to be found in the Castle of Wonders. This was the adventure that Gawain was to undertake, although for the time being he had to set out on an entirely different enterprise.

At this point Gawain had come to Parzival's aid, and from now on for a while he is the leading character in the story; yet Parzival continues to play a part behind the scenes. After Kondrie's departure, another visitor, a famous warrior Kingrimursel, entered the hall and proceeded to accuse Gawain of having slain his overlord. In spite of both Arthur's and Gawain's denial of this accusation, the newcomer declared that the only way for Gawain to clear himself would be to accept a challenge within 40 days in the kingdom of Schamfanzon, where the crime had occurred.

Thus the two most famous knights were driven at the same time to leave Arthur's court.

Through Kondrie, Arthur for the first time was made aware of Parzival's true name and lineage. There was general sorrow at his departure and the maiden Kunnewaaré, whom he had served so faithfully, herself armed him. We see in their relationship an example of the troubadour ideal of noble love, free from all possibility of physical consummation. It was Parzival that Kunnewaaré loved, but she knew that she was not destined to win him as her husband. The defeated Klamidé sought her hand in marriage and asked for Parzival's aid. In response to the latter's intercession, Kunnewaaré accepted the King who had been sent to do homage to her. Then, as the story tells us, there was a sad parting between the two who had such affection for each other.

Gawain in his farewell asked that God might help him some day to serve Parzival as he would wish. But Parzival replied, 'Alas, what is God? If He were mighty He would never have imposed such disgrace on us both. Now I shall renounce his service.' He even told Gawain that women were more to be trusted than God.

Parzival had now to find a new relationship with the spiritual world. The winning of Kondwiramur had brought an end to the first period of his probation. His second was now completed. He had lived through experiences the Celts would well have understood, for he had suffered the loss of happiness and the grief of unsatisfied love and longing.

Book 7: Obilot

The next two books are concerned with the adventures of Gawain. At a first reading these might seem irrelevant but their light-hearted charm provides relief after the tragic events of Books 5 and 6. Through them we are also given a deeper insight into Gawain's character. Though of dauntless courage, he did not seek combat for the sake of fighting but to serve those who were in need of help. However, this very quality of sympathy often led him into being misunderstood.

Gawain set out for the kingdom of Schamfanzon but on the way

34

became involved in a quite different adventure. He entered a realm where violent and uncontrolled passions were let loose. He had to pass through certain tests before he would be able to undertake his true task, the freeing of those held in the enchantments of the Castle of Wonders.

King Meljanz of Liz, while still a child, was entrusted after the death of his father to a loyal vassal named Lippaut until he became of age. He fell in love with Lippaut's daughter Obie, but she mocked him, saying that she would not be satisfied with anyone less than an emperor. As soon as he was independent, the indignant Meljanz made war against Lippaut, intending to seize Obie by force.

When on his journey Gawain sought hospitality with Lippaut in the city of Beaurosch, he found the gates closed and the hostile army taking up its position outside the city; so his squires put up his tent just under the walls. Lippaut's wife and two daughters came out on the battlements to watch him. The spiteful Obie, who now felt herself in a false position, began to mock at him, telling her family that he was a merchant come to make profit out of the war. But the younger daughter Obilot, who was still a child, declared that she was sure he was a knight, as she had never before seen anyone so noble. Gawain overheard all her conversation. Obie, bent on mischief, now sent a message to the burgomaster to say that a swindler had established himself outside the walls and she thought his goods ought to be confiscated to pay their mercenaries. The burgomaster, hastening to investigate, came upon Gawain. He immediately recognized that this handsome stranger was no swindler but a noble knight, and so he sent word to Lippaut, who at once besought Gawain's help. Gawain replied that he was involved in an affair of honour which did not allow him to delay. However, he promised to consider the matter and give his answer by nightfall.

In the meanwhile little Obilot had taken matters into her own hands and all alone made her way to Gawain. Imitating the courtly language of the grown-up world, she asked him to become her knight. She offered him her love and said she was sure he would not fail to serve her. Gawain could not resist the child's innocent confidence in him. He remembered Parzival's saying that it was better to trust women than God, so he gave his promise that he would bear arms in her honour, and he clasped her little hands in his own.

Obilot knew that it was the fashion for ladies to give tokens to those who fought on their behalf and she wondered what gift to give him. She consulted her little friend Clauditte who offered her best doll. But when her father heard that Obilot had won Gawain's support, he was so delighted that he asked her mother to make her a beautiful silk dress so that Gawain could wear the right sleeve on his shield.

The next day a violent conflict took place. Knights were flung from their horses and many were slain or captured. Among the combatants there were two who were outstanding. In support of Lippaut, Gawain, mounted on Gringolet, a Grail horse given him by Orilus, seemed invincible. Wherever the contest was fiercest, he was in the midst, and he finally took King Meljanz prisoner. On the other side a strange knight in red armour was equally remarkable, and succeeded in capturing three of Lippaut's allies. Hearing that Meljanz was taken, the Red Knight knew that it was useless to continue the fight, so he sent his prisoners into Beaurosch to offer themselves in exchange for Meljanz. But he added that if they were unsuccessful they should seek for the Grail on his behalf. If they failed in this, they were to go to his wife in Pelrapar and tell her that he still yearned for her love. From now on he no longer sent defeated knights to Kunnewaaré but to Kondwiramur.

When Gawain heard this he knew that the Red Knight was none other than Parzival and he was grateful that fate had saved them from coming into conflict. Meljanz now deeply regretted that he had ever turned against Lippaut who had been as a second father to him. Gawain said to him, 'Here bonds must be joined anew which nothing but death can sever.' According to the custom of the time he presented his prisoner to Obilot and gave her the right to decide his fate. Obilot, realizing that Obie's treatment of Meljanz sprang from pride and a desire to test him, commanded them to come together, and the episode ended in a general reconciliation. The only sorrows were those of Obilot and Gawain. The little girl wept bitterly and begged to go with him, and, as he left, Gawain's heart was heavy with grief.

It seems at first surprising that Gawain and Parzival should have supported opposing sides, but we have to remember that they were following different destinies. Gawain's calling led him to protect those who were innocently attacked, but Parzival had to stand by those who were at fault in order to redeem them; hence we find him negotiating Meljanz's freedom. While in this adventure Gawain was dominant, he was riding on a Grail horse. But Parzival was mounted on Ingliat, Gawain's stallion, which had escaped during the conflict.

Book 8: Antikonie

In the following adventure Gawain again found himself involved in a quarrel which was not of his seeking. At last he reached the kingdom of Schamfanzon and came to the Castle of Askalon. King Vergulacht greeted him warmly but, as he himself was involved in some pressing affair, he asked his sister Antikonie to entertain Gawain until his return.

Antikonie was young and charming so that she and Gawain, happy in each other's company, began to exchange certain intimacies. An old knight became suspicious that the guest was about to seduce his master's sister, and he set up an indignant shouting. Servants came running and the cry was raised that the slayer of the former King of Schamfanzon was betraying Vergulacht.

Antikonie and Gawain now found themselves in the greatest danger for Gawain was completely unarmed and his squires had all gone off in chase of a sparrowhawk. She led the way to a tower where Gawain tore a bolt from the door and, with this as a weapon, threatened their assailants. In the meantime Antikonie had found a set of chessmen and began to hurl the heavy figures of kings, queens and knights, so that many of their attackers were stunned. At this moment Kingrimursel arrived on the scene. He immediately realized what was happening and was horrified. He had promised Gawain safe conduct and he alone was entitled to mete out vengeance. This unlawful attack would only bring him into disgrace, so he went to the support of Gawain.

When Vergulacht turned up he was tempted to continue the conflict which now also involved an attack on Kingrimursel, but the latter at last managed to make him see reason. Vergulacht was severely reproached by his sister for offending against the laws of hospitality, so at last a reconciliation was brought about. One of the terms of the agreement was that Gawain should take over a task from Vergulacht. In the wood the latter had met a knight in red armour who had defeated him but had granted him his life on condition he sought for the Grail; so Gawain now agreed to take over the task given by Parzival to Vergulacht. He then rode away to fulfil his duty but he was sad at heart at leaving the fair Antikonie.

We see in these last two adventures how Gawain was frequently misjudged. Obie wrongly accused him of being a merchant and then a swindler. The followers of Vergulacht attacked and might well have killed him on account of an unjustified suspicion. He was obliged to appear in Schamfanzon to defend himself for a crime he had never committed. However, since these episodes have a light note, the reader is not led into great anxiety on Gawain's account.

In the episode with Antikonie Gawain's natural sympathy for all women brought him into danger. In the future he would have to learn steadfastness through stern trials. In taking over Parzival's quest for the Grail he was led into accomplishing his own particular destiny.

Book 9: Trevrezent

The poet opens the ninth book with an appeal to Lady Adventure to comfort us that all goes well with Herzeleide's son, and we are led to hope that Parzival's long series of misfortunes may come to an end. This book contains the central theme of the whole story. Parzival now came to an all-important turning point in his development, for his meeting with the hermit Trevrezent brought a completely changed mood of soul, which enabled him to transform the qualities which he had so far acquired and prepare himself for his final achievement.

Since leaving Arthur's court, he travelled over land and sea and took part in many battles where he was always victorious. The sword, given him by Anfortas, had once snapped but had been rewelded at the magic spring. This implies that he had now learned the rightful use of this weapon.

While journeying one day through wild country, he came to a hermit's cell. He rode up to the window to ask the way, and to his surprise a woman came at his call. She wore a grey gown and a widow's band around her hair, while on her finger shone a little ring with a red garnet that flashed like fire. In reply to Parzival's comment that he did not know that a hermitess was allowed to wear a ring, she told him that she wore it in memory of her true love, who had been slain and was now buried in this shrine where she mourned over his grave. Then Parzival recognized his cousin Siguné and removed his helmet. 'Is it you, Sir Parzival?' she said. She no longer reproached him but asked how his quest had prospered. When Parzival told her of his sorrow at losing the Grail, she offered helpful advice. She told him he was now near Monsalvasch and that as Kondrie, who every Saturday brought her food for the week, had just ridden away, he might be able to follow her tracks through the wood.

Parzival set out, but, just as the tracks disappeared, he was challenged by a Grail knight who forbade him to penetrate further. A fierce fight ensued. They were just on the edge of a ravine which was concealed by the trees and ferns. In the onslaught the Templar lost his seat and rolled over the cliff. Parzival's horse, charging after him, also fell and, although Parzival saved himself by clinging to the branches overhead, he saw that his horse was killed. The Templar got up unhurt and made his escape but his mount was left free for Parzival to use. His meeting with Siguné had again brought him a step forward. Through following her guidance he had acquired a Grail horse.

It was early in the year and a light snow had fallen. Parzival had not ridden far when he came upon an aged knight with his wife and daughters who were walking as pilgrims barefoot through the snow. The old knight reproached Parzival for riding fully armed on a holy day, for it was Good Friday. Parzival replied that he had lost count of time and, as for it being a holy day, God had refused to help him so now he was doing without God.

The pilgrims asked Parzival to join them but he declined and said farewell. However, the knight's words and the daughters' sympathy had softened his stern mood and he cried aloud, 'If God

39

can help, then may He show this horse the way.' He let the reins fall loosely and the Grail horse guided him to the cell of Trevrezent, where long ago he had sworn Jeschuté's innocence. In humbled mood he approached through the snow and addressed the hermit with the words, 'Sir, give me counsel, I am one who has sinned.' He was led into a cave where a fire was glowing and where he could remove his cold armour and warm his limbs, while his horse was taken to shelter under the protection of the cliff.

This episode comes as the climax of the entire story for here at last Parzival found peace after his long quest. In reply to his complaint that God had deserted him, Trevrezent warned him of the sin of Lucifer who had set himself up against God. He then told him of the loss of Paradise and described how, when Cain slew his brother, the blood of Abel defiled the ground so that the earth lost her innocence. Through Cain's sin hatred was stirred up among men, the animals were taught to destroy one another and the plant world was tainted with poison. The love of Christ, who gave His life for man, was the only power which could bring redemption, and so man must seek to serve the Christ and make atonement to the one who had entered the dark earth as a brightly shining light. In his *Parsifal*, Wagner expresses most beautifully in music the Good Friday mood when the world of nature rejoices in its redemption.

Trevrezent proceeded to teach Parzival about the Grail. Although Eschenbach does not openly refer to this, one of the medieval conceptions of the Grail was that it had once shone as the brightest jewel in Lucifer's crown. When Lucifer was cast out of heaven he lost this stone and it was brought to earth by angels. We can see that in this Imagination the Grail is represented as the bearer of heavenly powers freed from the influence of Lucifer.

Titurel had built a castle as a temple to guard the Grail Mysteries and had gathered round him a group of Knights Templars. Only those whose names were proclaimed in the stars were called to its service. Within the castle only the Grail King was allowed to marry, but when any neighbouring country was left without an heir, a Grail knight would be sent to give guidance and was then free to take a wife. The daughters of the King married into ruling families so that the influence of the Grail wisdom was spread abroad.

Titurel was now too old to serve as King though he was still able to give wise counsel. His life was sustained by the Grail which had the power to consume the phoenix to ashes but immediately to restore it anew. On Good Friday a dove came down from heaven to lay a white wafer on the stone, thus renewing its life-giving strength.

Anfortas, Titurel's grandson, had become King, but he had not been faithful to his calling. After he had received his dreadful wound, Trevrezent, who had also indulged in love quests, retired to a hermit's cell to do penance for his brother's sin. The Grail knights had long lived in hope, remembering the promise that a young knight would come to their relief, but a foolish lad had found his way to the castle and failed to ask what ailed the King. Now they had all lost heart.

Trevrezent then enquired into Parzival's parentage and it emerged that he also belonged to the Grail family. Both Herzeleide and Siguné's mother Schoysiane were the sisters of Anfortas and Trevrezent, so Siguné's relationship with the Grail community is made clear. Parzival now learned of his two great errors. Through leaving his mother, he had brought about her death. Ither of Gaheviess, whom he had so light-heartedly slain, was his cousin. He had committed the twofold sin of Cain. Since leaving Arthur's court, Parzival had, like the pre-Christian Nordic hero, followed his life of adventure with defiant pride; now he had to bear the heavy burden of guilt.

For a while he did not mention that he himself had been the fool who had found his way to the Grail Castle. Sad at heart the two men paused in their talk and went out to seek their meal of roots and herbs in the snow-clad woods. On their return Parzival begged his uncle to have mercy on him and tell him what to do, for he was the knight who had failed to heal the King.

Trevrezent was deeply grieved but he realized Parzival's need of help. He warned him that it was useless to seek for the Grail for it appeared only to those who were divinely chosen, but he should fulfil his knightly duties in the knowledge that God accepted all earnest service.

Parzival stayed 15 days in the hermit's cell and Trevrezent's teaching of the Redeemer sank into his heart. When they parted Trevrezent absolved him with the words, 'Give your sins to me. In the sight of God I am the guarantee for your atonement.' He was able to do for Parzival what he had not achieved for Anfortas. He himself in his youth had deserted the Grail in quest of love adventures and so was powerless to help his brother, but Parzival's steadfast striving had awakened in Trevrezent a new gift of blessing.

In the course of his adventures Parzival had developed those qualities which had been prepared in pre-Christian days by the Greeks, the Celts and the Nordic people. But he was now able to imbue them with a new life for he had found his relationship with the being of the Christ.

Book 10: Orgelusé

In Book 10 we return once more to the story of Gawain. His adventures in attaining the rulership of the Castle of Wonders are like a reflection or a picture in reverse of those of Parzival in connection with the Grail. The Grail Castle revealed itself only to those who were chosen, while the Castle of Wonders was easy to find but the ones who came under its spell were not free to leave. Four hundred knights served the Grail and four hundred ladies were held captive in the Castle of Wonders. The one who attended the Grail ceremony was required to ask a question, but the one approaching the Castle of Wonders was warned that the asking of a question was full of danger.

At the end of Book 8 we discovered how on Parzival's behalf Gawain had taken over from Vergulacht the quest of the Grail. As he rode on his way he came upon a woman weeping over a wounded knight. Gawain was skilled in the art of healing and immediately offered his help. He saw that the knight's wound was not mortal but he was bleeding internally so that the blood was pressing on the heart. He stripped the bark from a linden twig and, making a little tube, gave it to the woman to suck so that the blood would flow outward. Then he bound the wound with her scarf. Recovering consciousness, the knight said that he had been attacked and wounded near the city of Logrois by an enemy,

Lischois Giwellius, who had then taken his horse. Gawain at once set out to overtake and punish the offender.

When he drew near the city of Logrois he was struck by its appearance. High above the town rose the citadel, but to the observer it seemed to be endlessly spinning like a top so that no enemy could easily take it. Below the fortress were fruit trees in great profusion and the inhabitants seemed to be celebrating some festival with music and dancing. However, before he crossed the bridge into the town, Gawain became aware that sitting beside a spring was the most beautiful woman he had ever seen. This was Orgelusé, the Duchess of Logrois. Gawain approached her with reverence and asked if he might be accepted as her knight. She replied with great scorn that she saw no reason why he could expect such an honour and, if he served her, he would certainly get no reward. Gawain was not to be discouraged; he was willing to endure any treatment she bestowed on him for, he said, he did not wish to receive love unearned. She then ordered him to go and fetch her horse which he would find in the orchard beyond the bridge.

When Gawain entered the town and passed among the singers and dancers, they stopped to warn him that he should have nothing to do with Orgelusé as she had brought many men to their doom. But in spite of their well-meant advice Gawain secured the horse and brought it to its mistress. She thanked him with the words, 'Welcome, you goose.' Then she mounted and set off across the heath with Gawain following.

Presently Gawain dismounted to gather a herb. He explained to her that this had power to heal a wounded knight for whom he had been caring. Orgelusé replied scornfully that if he were a doctor as well as a knight he would certainly do well for a living.

At that moment Orgelusé's squire, Malcreature, came to her with a message. He was hideously ugly, with a face like a dog and two great boar's tusks, for he was none other than Kondrie's brother. However, instead of having long braided eyebrows and tresses, his hair was like the bristles of a hedgehog. He was so rude that Gawain struck him, thereby cutting his hand on the sharp bristles, at which Orgelusé laughed maliciously, saying, 'I love to see you both so furious.'

They soon came upon the wounded knight and his lady. The

knight declared that he was now much better and asked Gawain to help them both onto the lady's horse so that he could be taken to a neighbouring hospital to recover. But while Gawain was helping the lady to mount, the knight saw his chance. He leapt onto Gawain's horse and galloped away. But, before riding out of earshot, he shouted back that he was now having his revenge for an insult Gawain had made him suffer years ago at Arthur's court. Gawain now recognized Urian, a knight who had been condemned to death for assaulting a lady. Gawain had pleaded for his life, and the death sentence was commuted to the punishment of living and eating for a month with the dogs in their kennels. Although Gawain had saved his life, Urian had borne him implacable hatred as being the cause of his degradation.

Now, to Orgelusé's great amusement, Gawain was without a mount and so had to make do with Malcreature's horse which was lame and stumbled at every step. Gawain bore her insults and told her that the more she mocked him now the more she would wish to compensate later.

At last they came to a river and beyond it they saw a lordly castle with battlements and towers. At the windows Gawain saw so many ladies that he thought there must be at least four hundred. A ferryman was waiting at the waterside to take them across. But before they reached the boat, a knight came charging down upon them. It was none other than Lischois Giwellius whom Gawain had been seeking. The two knights were at once engaged in fierce combat. At the first charge Gawain's wretched nag collapsed, but Lischois Giwellius also lost his seat, and the fight ended in a wrestling match in which Gawain was finally the victor. To his surprise he found that his opponent's horse which he had now won was his own steed Gringolet stolen by Urian. Gawain was hoping for Orgelusé's approval of his prowess, but, while the two heroes were fighting, she had stepped into the ferryman's boat and been taken across the river.

The ferryman, realizing that Gawain was cast down by Orgelusé's desertion, invited him to be his guest for the night. He told him that Klingsor was the lord of this domain and master of the Chateau Merveil. Under his sway the rule of life was 'sad today and glad tomorrow'.

Whereas Parzival when invited by the Fisher King to the Grail Castle was sumptuously entertained, Gawain in the ferryman's home received but scanty fare. He was offered salad in vinegar and three roasted larks, one of which he was asked to give to the ferryman's wife in reward for her service. But whereas Parzival spent the night disturbed by terrible dreams, Gawain slept untroubled until early morning.

Book 11: Arnivé

Gawain woke early to the sound of birdsong. He went to the window to listen and found that he had a view of the castle which he had seen the evening before, and there were the many ladies walking to and fro in the great hall. He was astonished that they were not still asleep as the day had hardly dawned.

When the ferryman's daughter Bené came to attend to him, he asked who the ladies were. 'Sir,' she said, 'do not ask. I cannot tell you anything.' When he pressed her for some answer, she began to cry. Presently her father came in and, when he heard the cause of her tears, he said, 'For God's sake do not ask! Over there is misery beyond all misery.' But Gawain persisted, 'You must tell me. I shall find out anyway what is going on up there.'

His host then explained to him that if he entered the Chateau Merveil he would have to experience the Wonder Bed and face death. There would be little chance of his coming out alive. Gawain expressed his determination to face whatever perils were in store if he could bring some consolation to those who were held by enchantment.

The ferryman then offered his help. He said that if Gawain survived he would become ruler of the kingdom, but, if he died, it would be the greatest grief that could befall them. He then mentioned that the previous day he had ferried the slayer of Ither of Gaheviess across the river. Gawain realized that Parzival was once more near him, but he learned that the Red Knight had heard nothing of the story of the Castle of Wonders so had not attempted this adventure.

Gawain's armour was brought to him and his host lent him an

especially stout shield, warning him that he must on no account part either with it or his sword. He told him that he could not take his horse with him into the castle but he must leave it with a merchant who had set up a booth just outside the gate. The family all wept as Gawain took his departure and he promised them, 'If God permits, I shall not fail to repay you for the hospitality you have shown me.'

When Gawain arrived at the gate he found the merchant in charge of a great silk tent filled with marvellous treasures. He enquired about some small items of jewellery within his means, but the merchant said, 'If you succeed in your enterprise everything I have will belong to you.' He readily took Gawain's horse into care. The horse often appears as an image of the intelligence, as in the story of the wooden horse that was devised to win an entry into Troy. We can interpret his leaving his horse as a sign that he could not in the Castle of Wonders make use of the intelligence which guided him in everyday life.

Having passed through the gate, Gawain saw many towers rising above the ramparts and there, in front of him, was the great hall with its vaulted arches and its roof as brightly coloured as peacocks' plumes. The ladies were no longer to be seen. At one end of the hall was a door standing open, leading into a chamber with a pavement that shone as glass. In the centre stood the Wonder Bed on its swift wheels of four red rubies. Gawain knew that he had to mount it but, from whatever angle he approached, it shot off in the opposite direction. He gave a mighty leap and landed in the middle. The bed at once began to rush round wildly, slamming into each wall with a crash like thunder. Gawain lay still and committed himself to God's care. Presently from a gallery above there came a volley of great rocks, followed by a flight of powerful arrows. Gawain had the greatest difficulty in protecting himself with the ferryman's shield, and, although it well withstood the bombardment, he was bruised with the blows and the arrows did not entirely miss him. He became dizzy with the movement and the noise. Suddenly the bed came to rest. A door opened and a rough-looking fellow, clothed completely in fishskin and carrying a great club, entered the room. He said angrily, 'It's only by the devil's power that you are still alive. I will see that you now forfeit your life.' As he retreated a sound like the roll of 20 drums could be heard and a husky lion as great as a horse rushed into the room.

Gawain leapt to the floor and stood on his guard, but at the first lunge the lion ripped through his shield with its claws. Gawain, with a sweep of his sword, cut off one of the lion's legs. There was a rush of blood. As the fight continued the combatants were slipping about in the flood. The lion leapt again and again and tried to drag Gawain to the ground, but at last with a bold stroke the hero pierced it to the heart.

By now Gawain was seriously wounded and dizzy from loss of blood. He sank unconscious onto the lion's body. However, from above the aged Queen Arnivé, mother of King Arthur, had watched the contest. She saw with joy the death of the lion but feared that Gawain had also lost his life. She sent two of her attendants down to examine the wounded knight and find out if he were still alive. They carefully removed his helmet and watched to see if he was breathing, but there seemed no sign of movement. Then one of the maidens lifted the fur edging of his tunic and held it to his nose. There was a faint flutter which showed that he still breathed, so, forcing her ring between his teeth, she poured a little water into his mouth. This restored him to consciousness. Then Queen Arnivé brought salves and ointments and bandaged his 50 wounds. When a bed had been prepared and a fire kindled, she placed a herb in his mouth so that he fell asleep and slept soundly until evening.

The whole experience which Gawain had endured was a test of his ability to control his all too susceptible feeling life. We are shown in imaginative pictures his awareness of the physiological processes at work in our breathing and blood circulation. These normally do not rise into consciousness and are felt only under conditions of disturbance caused by illness or violent feelings of passionate excitement or anger. Although Gawain had survived the wild movements of the Wonder Bed and had slain the lion, he had not fully achieved the control of his passions. In certain early Rosicrucian drawings it appears that the fight with the lion should end with the mastery, not with the death, of the creature. As Gawain had only partially succeeded he would still have to face further trials.

Book 12: Eidegast

The twelfth book opens with a description of the power of Frau Minne, the Lady Love honoured by the troubadours. We are told that Gawain had always given her his true service and many of his relatives connected with Arthur's court are also mentioned as being under her spell.

Gawain spent the night after his adventure tossing in anguish because of his unrequited love for Orgelusé, and his restless movements loosened the bandages so that his wounds bled afresh. However, at dawn he found clean garments laid out for him so that he was able to appear in fitting attire.

He now began to explore the castle and found that at one end of the hall a winding staircase led up to a narrow tower high above the castle roof. In the centre stood a circular pillar that reflected all the lands around. Gawain began to watch the images appearing in the mirror. There were people, riding, running and walking, and the great mountains in the background seemed to collide with reverberating sounds. Gawain received an impression of the same restless movements that he had experienced on the preceding day.

While he was observing the changing pictures, Queen Arnivé, accompanied by her daughter Sangivé, who was Gawain's mother, and by his two sisters, Itonjé and Kondrie, came to greet him. They did not recognize him for he had left his family at a very young age to be reared in Arthur's court.

Arnivé described to Gawain the properties of the pillar which had been stolen by Klingsor from the Eastern Queen Sekundille whom we later learn to be the lover of Feirefis. No hammer or smith could harm it and it reflected everything in a radius of six miles around. It seems to have had the quality of reflecting whatever the beholder wished to see, for Gawain now beheld across the river Orgelusé riding in the company of an attentive knight. Gawain, fearing that he was being deceived, turned to Arnivé for confirmation. When he heard that the lady mirrored in the pillar was indeed the beautiful Duchess of Logrois, he at once decided to go and attack her companion in order to win honour in her service. Arnivé begged him to desist as he was in no condition to undertake such a conflict—but it was impossible to restrain him.

The ladies wept, for it seemed certain that Gawain would be

defeated. He was so sorely wounded that he could scarcely carry his shield. However, mounting Gringolet, he made his way to the ferryman who furnished him with a strong spear and took him across the river.

In spite of the strength and courage of his opponent, known as the Turkoite, Gawain, with a masterly stroke, unseated him and became the victor. Orgelusé again greeted him with scornful words. She said that he was no doubt pleased that the ladies in the castle had been able to watch his success; however, as he had been so badly wounded, she was sure that his shield was like a sieve, and he would be only too ready to avoid the combat she would ask of him if he really wished to serve her. Gawain replied that her favour would bring healing to his wounds and that there was no adventure so dangerous that he would not undertake it on her behalf.

Orgelusé now ordered him to leap the Ford Perilous and win for her a wreath from the tree guarded by King Gramoflanz who had caused her the deepest grief. She allowed him the favour of riding by her side through Klingsor's forest until they heard the roar of a waterfall and came to a ravine across which they could see the tree from which the wreath was to be gathered. Here Orgelusé waited to watch the result.

Gawain at once spurred on his horse to take the leap. Gringolet reached the other side with only his two front feet and fell back into the stream where he was swept down by the swift current. Orgelusé, seeing their danger, burst into tears. Gawain managed to cling to an overhanging branch and clutch his spear which was floating near him. He climbed out onto the bank and turned to rescue his horse. Gringolet was struggling, sometimes with his head above water, sometimes submerged, but at last the current carried him into a whirlpool near the bank. Gawain managed to reach the reins with his spear and guided the horse into the shallows.

He was now able to climb the bank and pluck a branch from the tree. But as he placed the wreath in his helmet, a handsome knight, wearing a hat decked with peacock feathers and a green silk cloak trimmed with ermine, rode up and challenged him. This was none other than King Gramoflanz, the owner of the tree.

The King informed Gawain that he knew Orgelusé had driven him to this deed in revenge because he had slain her husband

Eidegast. Gramoflanz had in recompense offered to make her his queen, but she had scorned him and sought his death.

Though Gramoflanz demanded recompense for the theft of his wreath, he declined to fight with Gawain. It was his custom never to fight with less than two adversaries at once, so he suggested that Gawain could make amends by doing him a favour. Though he had never seen her, he had fallen in love with Gawain's sister, Itonjé, so Gawain could be a go-between and take a little ring to her as a token of affection. Gawain agreed, but in the course of their conversation it emerged that there was one knight with whom Gramoflanz was prepared to fight in single combat. This was none other than Gawain himself whose fame made him a worthy opponent. Moreover, Gawain's father Lot had slain Gramoflanz's father, so there was a blood feud to be settled between them. When Gawain revealed his identity, the two agreed to meet and fight it out on the Plain of Ioflanz in eight days' time.

Gawain made the return leap with complete success. Orgelusé now fell at his feet and with tears offered her love, but Gawain imagined that she was still mocking him. He now showed that through his latest adventure he had at last mastered his passion and could meet her as an independent being. 'Lady,' he said, 'accept this wreath, but never again use your beauty to bring dishonour on any knight. If I must endure your mockery, I would rather renounce your love.'

Orgelusé, weeping bitterly, told him her story. She had once been happily married to Eidegast, a knight whom no man surpassed in honour; but he was slain by King Gramoflanz. Seeking an avenger to bring about the King's death, she had accepted the services of Anfortas, King of the Grail. To win her favour, Anfortas had presented her with the rich booth which stood outside the gate of the Castle of Wonders. But this whole realm had fallen under the power of Klingsor and, when Anfortas received his terrible wound while fighting for her, Orgelusé gave the booth to Klingsor as a bribe so that he should not harm them further.

We can only assume that Klingsor had thrown his spell over Orgelusé so that she bewitched all men who came into contact with her and drove them to injury or death. One knight alone had been able to withstand her. Orgelusé told Gawain that a Red Knight had come riding through her kingdom of Logrois. She had offered him her love but he had rejected her, saying that he had a more beautiful wife of his own. It is clear from this that Parzival had passed through Klingsor's kingdom but that the evil spell had no power over him.

Parzival's rejection now enabled Gawain to win Orgelusé. This theme bears a resemblance to the legend of Gawain and the Loathly Lady. In that story a beautiful maiden had been bewitched so that she appeared as a hideous hag. Through his courtesy in accepting her as his wife, Gawain had removed the spell. In Eschenbach's poem, Orgelusé does not appear ugly in feature, but she is under a spell to mislead and destroy so that she drove many men to their doom. Through his patient service to her and his final freeing of himself from her power, Gawain was able to redeem her. From now on she appeared as a good and gracious Queen.

This book ends with the account of Gawain sending a letter to King Arthur to report the forthcoming encounter with Gramoflanz and to invite all the court of the Round Table to the Plain of Ioflanz to support him in his final trial. He still kept the inhabitants of the Castle of Wonders ignorant of his name and title. Queen Arnivé tried to find out from the messenger the contents of the letter, but he was faithful to Gawain's instructions and her curiosity remained unsatisfied.

Book 13: Klingsor

It is only in the thirteenth book that Gawain is represented as the real master of the Castle of Wonders. Until his winning of the wreath of Gramoflanz all were waiting to see whether he would be able to complete his victory and bring the power of Klingsor to an end. With the redemption of Orgelusé he was now acknowledged by all as their lord. There was a grand festival of feasting and dancing. The knights whom Gawain had conquered, Lischois Giwellius and the Turkoite, now named as Florant of Itolac, were greeted as friends and, as a compliment to Orgelusé, freed without conditions.

Gawain now set about fulfilling his promise to Gramoflanz. He found out from Bené, the ferryman's daughter, which of the ladies was his sister Itonjé and then, without revealing his relationship, he sat by her. With kindly interest he showed her the ring and questioned her whether she had yet loved any knight. She was led to confess that, though she had never seen him, she loved Gramoflanz. In answer to her plea Gawain offered his help, but he did not reveal that he was her brother.

We are told that as night approached the hall was hung with candles but, even if no candles had been present, darkness would have been dispelled, for Orgelusé shed around her the radiance of the day.

The feasting and dancing continued well into the night until Arnivé warned Gawain that he still needed rest as his wounds were not yet fully healed. Orgelusé undertook to care for him and the poet implies that what took place between them belonged to the realm of the mysteries. Love brought the power of healing.

In the meantime Gawain's messenger was on his way to Arthur's court. When he presented the letter, there was a general rejoicing as the King and Queen had heard nothing of their favourite nephew for more than four and a half years. They undertook to be present when Gawain met Gramoflanz on the Plain of Ioflanz. Only Kay was displeased and grumbled that Gawain would probably have disappeared by the time they reached the appointed place for he frisked about like a squirrel and was gone before anyone could catch him.

The lord of the Castle of Wonders had to accept and bring into harmony the rhythmic interplay of joy and sorrow. While everyone was waiting for Gawain's contest with Gramoflanz, Queen Arnivé taught him about the power and character of Klingsor and what had been achieved through Gawain's victory. Klingsor, the lord of Terra Labur, came from a family of famous magicians and had attained universal renown. He succeeded in winning the love of Iblis, wife of Ibert, King of Sicily. When Ibert discovered their guilt he took his revenge. He castrated Klingsor, who then becoming embittered, gave up his life to the study of black magic so that he might acquire unrivalled power. He won the service of both good and evil spirits, for none could withstand him unless they had the special protection of God. He was granted the rulership of the Castle of Wonders as a bribe from a king who wished to be left in peace. Now Gawain had become lord of his domain and of all Klingsor's captives, whether heathen or Christian. Arnivé advised Gawain to allow all who wished to return to their own countries.

The Queen concluded by saying, 'May He who has counted the stars teach you to give us help and turn our grief to joy.' She compared the alternation of grief and joy to water becoming ice and then once more being freed from its fetters. It has been mentioned that the members of the Arthurian cult were dedicated to bringing the harmony of the heavens into the ordering of affairs on earth. This was Gawain's task as its leading representative.

At last Arthur and his mighty host arrived on the Plain of Ioflanz and countless handsome tents were set up. Gawain was moved to tears at the sight, for he had been brought up by Arthur and their love for each other was true and steadfast. There had been some confusion on the way as the followers of Orgelusé, imagining that a hostile army was approaching, had launched an attack. Gawain had failed to report what was happening as he had wished everyone to be duly impressed with the magnificence of Arthur's retinue. However, the skirmish was soon over and Gawain prepared a fitting welcome.

A great fleet of ships crossed the river. The magnificent booth from the Castle of Wonders was set up on the plain. Then a procession of knights and ladies rode into Arthur's camp, so that his tents were completely encircled by Gawain's followers. The King and Queen came forward to give them all a royal greeting. Arthur was reunited with his mother, his sister and his two nieces. Finally Gawain led him to Orgelusé, Duchess of Logrois, and Arthur and Guinevere were made aware of all that he had achieved. There was universal joy. Only Kay was mocking; he marvelled where Gawain had found this swarm of women.

Gawain made sure that everyone was provided with all comforts required for the night, as on the following morning the combat was to take place. He himself rose very early to practise his skill in arms and to make certain that his wounds were sufficiently healed for him to fight freely. As he was riding alone across the plain he saw an armed knight approaching.

Book 14: Gramoflanz

Gawain took note that the knight riding towards him was wearing a wreath from the tree where he himself had plucked a branch for Orgelusé. He assumed that the stranger was Gramoflanz, who must also have come early to the trysting place; so without delay he prepared for combat. Soon both were fighting with powerful strokes and the ground was strewn with splinters. But according to the poet, whoever won would suffer sorrow.

In the meantime King Arthur had sent a deputation to Gramoflanz asking him, in consideration of the esteem in which the Arthurian court was held, to forego the fight with Gawain. However, the messengers found the King in an arrogant mood, determined on the combat. He had just received a love token from Itonjé and was above all anxious to distinguish himself to win her favour. In great splendour he set out for the place of meeting.

On their return journey Arthur's messengers came upon Gawain and his opponent in their deadly conflict. In alarm they cried out Gawain's name, for they saw that he was near the end of his strength. When the strange knight heard their cry, he suddenly threw his sword away and exclaimed, 'I am dishonoured to have taken part in this contest. Alas, that I should have fought with the noble Gawain! It is I myself I have vanquished.'

The stranger revealed himself as Parzival. Gawain replied, 'Your hand gained the victory. Now you may grieve, for if your heart knows truth faith, it is yourself that you have conquered.'

Then Gawain felt a roaring in his head and sank fainting to the ground. Running to him, Arthur's squires began to fan him to restore consciousness. At this moment there came towards them the three armies of Arthur, of Orgelusé, and of Klingsor's host now under the leadership of Gawain, all in preparation for the coming combat. When Gramoflanz also arrived on the scene he was greatly disturbed to find that everything had gone contrary to his plans. Gawain was obviously in no condition now to fulfil their undertaking, so he offered to postpone their contest until the next day.

Parzival greeted Gramoflanz courteously and offered to take Gawain's place, but the King replied that this battle was essentially between himself and Gawain, who owed tribute for the wreath he had plucked for Orgeluse. As King Arthur's army rode back to their encampment, Parzival was at first diffident about appearing before the court where he had previously suffered the disgrace of Kondrie's curse. But Arthur welcomed him with the assurance that the fame of his deeds had reached them to wipe out any doubts they might have had of his nobility.

Gawain especially treated him with courtesy and ordered for him fresh clothing of the richest quality. It was painful for Orgeluse when she was asked to greet with a kiss the one who had rejected her offer of love, but she obeyed Gawain's request. The rest of the day passed pleasantly for all concerned.

The following morning Gramoflanz was determined that this time there should be no mistake, so he arrived early on the field. He was vexed that Gawain was not already there, but presently a knight in full armour rode forward and began the attack.

Meanwhile Gawain was attending Mass in the company of Arthur and his court. When the service was over they rode towards the appointed place and on the way were astonished to hear the clash of arms. They arrived on the scene to find Gramoflanz in sore distress. He had hitherto scorned to fight with only one adversary, but now his opponent seemed to have the strength of six. The arrogant King was humbled in his self-esteem. When Arthur's army appeared he realized that again a mistake had been made; he had been engaged with the stranger knight and had been worsted. Now it was Gawain's turn to offer a postponement until the following day.

During the afternoon events were taking place behind the scenes. Itonjé was overcome with grief to realize it was her lover and brother who were to meet in battle. Arnivé took her to Arthur and she pleaded with him to prevent the fight. Arthur sought counsel with the uncle of Gramoflanz and between them they persuaded Itonjé and Orgeluse to use their influence. Orgeluse, for love of Gawain, should renounce her hatred of Gramoflanz; Itonjé should convince Gramoflanz that his love for her could not be rewarded if he slew her brother. Through their intercession the warriers were reconciled and Arthur then gave Itonjé in marriage to the one she loved.

The conclusion of this conflict between Gramoflanz and Gawain may seem something of an anticlimax. A crisis had developed and then dissolved away. We need to consider these events a little more deeply. At the time of the height of the Arthurian cult knights did not fight for individual glory. However, at the time of these happenings, the order was beginning to decline and the conduct of both Ither of Gaheviess and Gramoflanz show that they were much occupied with their personal prestige. Both Parzival and Gawain had won a wreath from the tree of Gramoflanz—a sign that they were superseding him in leadership. Gramoflanz claimed the right to fight with Gawain, partly on account of a blood feud, but in the post-Christian era the carrying on of family conflicts in this way was an anachronism. Parzival now appeared on the scene to prevent a misfortune. From the time of his trance at the sight of the blood drops until his meeting with Trevrezent he had been under the influence of Gawain, but now he had regained control of his own destiny. He was therefore able to direct both Gawain and Gramoflanz so that this unnecessary conflict should not bring tragedy.

We need to take note of the words spoken by Parzival and Gawain when they discovered that they had been fighting each other. Parzival said, 'It is myself I have vanquished.' And Gawain replied, 'It is yourself that you have conquered.' They recognized their interdependence. In the modern age the human being cannot rely on his own strength alone; he needs to unite his forces at the right moment with others who are developing spiritual consciousness.

At the marriage festival of Gramoflanz and Itonjé there was general rejoicing. All dangers and difficulties now seemed overcome. Klingsor's power was at an end, the ladies were freed from his spell, Gawain was lord of the Castle of Wonders and all conflict was brought to rest. Parzival alone felt an outsider. He was still separated from his dearly loved wife and it was impossible for him to think of paying court to another. He realized that there was still some task in store for him, so in the early dawn he armed himself and stole away with the thought, 'May Fortune show me what would be best for me to do.'

Book 15: Feirefis

As Parzival was travelling through a great forest he came to a bright glade. Here he met a powerful knight clad in the richest armour and trappings that he had ever seen. His surcoat was flashing with jewels and above his helmet there rose a talisman in the form of a strange beast known as an ecidemon. The two warriors at once rushed into combat. Shields were pierced with spears, and splinters flew, but neither lost his seat, so at length they leapt to the ground to fight it out with swords.

The mighty stranger kept shouting his war-cry of 'Trabonet', the name of the pagan land from whence he came, and Parzival found himself being driven back. Then he mustered his strength and, concentrating all his thoughts on his wife and on the Grail, he cried, 'Pelrapar.' The ecidemon was shattered with blows and the heathen sank to his knees. But at that moment Parzival's sword, which he had won from the Red Knight, broke in his hand and he was left unarmed. The last of his early debts was now paid and he had to prepare for death.

The heathen leapt to his feet, but he courteously withdrew from the fight, saying, 'Brave man, I should win no renown by attacking you when you have no sword. Let there be a truce between us.' The stranger suggested that they should reveal their names and titles and he declared himself a member of the royal house of Angevin. This astonished Parzival who was by right of birth the ruler of Anjou but, remembering the description of the heathen queen at Arthur's court, he asked his companion whether he had a complexion like a parchment with writing on it, black on a white ground. The stranger removed his helmet and showed his skin which was like the magpie's plumage. He was none other than Parzival's half-brother Feirefis.

The two brothers took great joy in each other and Feirefis said, 'You have fought here against yourself; against yourself I rode into combat. Your strength helped us so that it prevented our deaths.'

We have here a similar claim to that made by Gawain. These three characters were complementary to one another. Whereas Parzival guided his life through his conscious ideals and Gawain by his sensitive feelings, Feirefis acted out of his will impulses. Hence each was able to assist the other in times of crisis.

Parzival now learned that his brother had a mighty army waiting for him at a neighbouring harbour, but they were so well disciplined that they would wait for months without deserting their posts. Feirefis wanted Parzival to go with him and he offered him a kingdom in the East, but Parzival suggested that first of all they should visit Arthur's court so that his brother could learn something of the chivalry of the West.

Just at that moment two knights came riding up. The fight between Feirefis and Parzival had been witnessed in the pillar of the Castle of Wonders. When this was reported to Gawain and Arthur they immediately assumed that Parzival must be one of the combatants and sent the knights to find out what was happening. The brothers were at once conducted to Gawain's and Arthur's camps.

Feirefis was received with great courtesy by all who had assembled for Gramoflanz's wedding. Everyone was astonished at the splendour of his armour and the richness of his garments which were thickly inlaid with jewels. The poet contrasts the wealth of Eastern warriors with the poverty of many Western knights.

The following morning, after Mass had been celebrated, a visitor was seen approaching. It was none other than Kondrie, the Messenger of the Grail. But this time she had not come to drive Parzival away. She prostrated herself before him and begged his forgiveness for her earlier harshness. She had now come to announce that his name was proclaimed in the stars as Lord of the Grail. Sorrow was to be transformed into joy, for the misery of Anfortas would be brought to an end and the Grail henceforth be truly served. Kondwiramur, with the two sons, Kardeiss and Lohengrin, who had been born after Parzival's departure, had been summoned to meet her husband. Parzival was told that one companion could accompany him to the Grail Castle, so Feirefis was his choice.

Before departing, Feirefis sent a message to his army to supply him with treasures from his store so that all present should receive rich gifts. Many a knight was helped to restore his fortunes.

As the brothers set out on their journey the word went round that no man by fighting could win the Grail; only those to whom it revealed itself could behold it and thus many who had set out on a vain search renounced their quest.

Book 16: Lohengrin

While Parzival was assured that at last his long quest had come to an end, Anfortas no longer knew how to bear his intolerable anguish. He cried out to his followers to spare him the sight of the Grail and allow him to die in peace. He even threatened that after death he would summon them before God's throne and denounce them for infidelity. But, aware of what the stars foretold, they would not obey him.

In the meantime, Kondrie was leading Parzival and Feirefis through the forest of Monsalvasch where a host of Grail knights was keeping guard. Feirefis was eager to attack and had to be restrained. When they recognized the turtle doves embroidered on Kondrie's garments, the Templars dismounted upon the grass to do homage to their deliverer. They felt that his greeting in return was a benediction.

The newcomers were led to the great hall where all were waiting in expectation. Anfortas greeted Feirefis courteously, then begged Parzival to come to his aid and, if nothing else availed, to allow him to die.

Parzival asked where the Grail was kept. After genuflecting before it, and praying that he might receive strength for his task, he asked, 'Uncle, what is it that ails you?' In a moment a change passed over the face of the Fisher King. The renewal of life and joy shone forth with a beauty surpassing that of all others present.

It may seem strange that the asking of a question could bring about a deed of healing. In ancient times there was a deep knowledge of the power that lived in words. Blessing and cursing were known to have effect, and even today in primitive tribes a curse can work with devastating strength. Through his many trials

Parzival had developed his capacities of judgement, of compassion and of steadfastness to a high degree, and, since his meeting with Trevrezent, he had united himself with the life-giving power of Christ. His words could now pour forth the forces of healing.

This event is differently expressed in Wagner's opera *Parsifal*, as, for a dramatic performance, a pictorial representation is more effective. Hence the healing act is there performed with the aid of the Holy Spear. This had originally belonged to the Grail King but through Anfortas's sin had fallen into Klingsor's hands. The rewinning of it was an outward sign of Parzival's stage of development. In his conversation with the pupils in the original Waldorf School, Rudolf Steiner showed how the knights of King Arthur were 'knights of the sword', whereas Parzival became a 'knight of the word'.

With the healing of Anfortas Parzival was acknowledged as King of the Grail. He now set out to meet his wife. Here followed one of the poet's most charming descriptions of human relationships. After visiting Trevrezent to tell him of the redemption of Anfortas, Parzival came early in the morning in the place where Kondwiramur, accompanied by her Uncle Kiot and her faithful retainers, had encamped for the night. Kiot led Parzival to the tent where the Queen was still asleep with her two young sons at her side. When she was roused to welcome her husband, the sorrow of their long parting was at an end. Many of the later events in the story are reflections of earlier ones. Parzival was reunited with his wife in the very place where nearly five years earlier he had been caught in a trance of longing when the red blood, the white snow and the dark trees had called up a vision of the one he so dearly loved.

Before Parzival could set out with his wife for the Grail Castle, Kardeiss, the elder of the twins, was crowned King of his parents' domains. Kiot took charge of his upbringing and he and the Queen's party returned to Pelrapar. When he grew to manhood, Kardeiss re-won those of his father's lands which had been wrongfully seized.

On their way to Monsalvasch Parzival wished to pay a last visit to Siguné. They came to the little hermitage and found her in an attitude of prayer above her lover's grave. But when they called to her they realized that she was dead. They broke into the cell and raised the stone under which her lover lay embalmed, as beautiful as he had been in life. They placed her there beside him; her long vigil now at an end. The impression is given that it was the presence of Parzival, the Grail King, that bestowed this beauty upon Anfortas whom he had healed and upon Schionatulander who had died for his sake.

In the evening after their arrival at the Grail Castle, the ritual procession took place and all were nourished by the Grail. Feirefis gazed in astonishment. He saw the maidens and the Grail-bearer and he received the choice food, but he could not see the Grail itself. Titurel was consulted and informed Parzival and Anfortas that only those who were baptized could behold the Grail. Feirefis fell passionately in love with Repanse de Schoie. He asked how he could win her, for he was prepared to undertake any dangerous battles on her behalf. When he was told that only if he became baptized as a Christian could he win her hand, he was completely prepared to take the step. After baptism he was able to see the Grail and all consented to his wedding with the bearer.

After 12 days of celebration Anfortas accompanied the young couple until Feirefis was reunited with his army. Here they received the news that the Queen Sekundille had died, so there was now no rival wife to create a problem for Repanse de Schoie. The son of Feirefis and his wife was Prester John through whom, according to legend, Christianity was firmly established in the East.

In the Feirefis episode we see how the task which Gamuret failed to achieve was fulfilled by Parzival. The poet makes it clear that many in the East were open to Christianity when it was presented in a suitable way. Belakane had been willing to become a Christian to keep her husband's love, but he had deserted her. Through Parzival's choice of his brother as his companion on his return to the Grail Castle, the link between West and East was brought about.

The story ends with a brief account of Parzival's son Lohengrin. Knights of the Grail were sometimes sent out into the world when a kingdom was left without leadership. Else, the young heiress of Brabant, was in danger. Her guardian was plotting to deprive her of her lands, so Lohengrin, who had by this time attained knighthood, was sent to her aid. Legend narrates that a swan brought him from the Grail Castle and he was accepted by the people of Brabant as their lord and Else's husband. However, he warned her that he could stay with her only if she never enquired into his true name and lineage. Her enemies began to spread false rumours until, through fear and uncertainty, she demanded to know his secret. Then the swan appeared and bore him back to the Kingdom of the Grail. However, he had restored Brabant to its position of leadership and he left behind a sword, a horn and a ring, symbols of the three kingly virtues of strength, wisdom and love.

This ending is important for, on the one hand, it implies that after Parzival's coming to leadership the virtue of the Grail did not remain enclosed within a select circle but rayed forth its influence into the world. On the other hand, Lohengrin became the inspirer of a newly rising culture, that of the free city states which were beginning to flourish at the close of the Middle Ages and which did so much to prepare the modern era.

PARZIVAL AS THE FORERUNNER OF MODERN MAN

There can be few serious-minded people today who are not deeply disturbed by the breakdown of nearly all hitherto accepted standards of human conduct. No government, even in the most highly developed countries, can control the outbreaks of corruption, cruelty and violence. Codes of honour, based on religious convictions or on pride in country, family or vocation, which at the beginning of this century provided a firm framework, have to a great extent disappeared, and in the struggle for self-advancement there is every sign of a general collapse of law and order.

Since the dawn of the modern age in the Renaissance, the right has gradually been won to make individual judgements on questions of religion, government and social relationships. But there are all too many signs that the ability to judge out of a true grasp of the situation is not widely developed. Personal opinions, inspired by egoism, fear or mass emotion, are often the decisive forces.

On the other hand, a strong element of idealism has existed in many of the struggles for independence. In the time of the French Revolution the watchwords of 'Liberty, Equality and Fraternity' seemed so inspiring that Wordsworth felt

> Bliss was it in that dawn to be alive,
> But to be young was very heaven.

Yet instead of the promised era of enlightenment there came the Reign of Terror. On the one hand abstract ideals were being proclaimed, while on the other animal passions ran wild. Although the waves of violence gradually subsided, there was never again the same respect for the traditions of the past.

During the nineteenth century the incredible developments in scientific research and technology gave rise to the conception that out of his own intelligence man was capable of solving all problems. The conviction arose that right planning could provide universal employment, comfortable living conditions and security against accident and old age. In fact an earthly Utopia could be established. There was also a widespread belief that, as men were fundamentally rational, once their material needs were satisfied there would be no temptation to violence and crime.

The last 50 years have proved these hopes to be illusory. If at the beginning of this century a seer had foretold the horrors of Hitler's death-camps or the destruction by Stalin of millions of his own people, no one would have believed him. It was impossible to imagine that evil could sweep with such overwhelming force over apparently civilized or pious people.

Through the two World Wars it also became clear that noble qualities were not displayed only by those whose material needs were being satisfied. The greatest courage was often shown by those who had lost everything. A supreme challenge aroused the determination never to yield to despair.

In the early Christian times man was considered to be a being of body, soul and spirit. But in the Ecumenical Council of AD 869 the spirit was brought into question in the Western Church. The individual human being had to rely on the offices of the priest to mediate between him and the spiritual world. During the nineteenth century even a true knowledge of the soul was lost. Typical of a widespread attitude was the statement of a famous surgeon that in the course of his operations he had explored every part of the human body but nowhere had he found any trace of a soul. Man came to be regarded as an object conditioned by heredity and environment. From this conception there developed a mechanical picture of life. Man's brain was likened to a tape-recorder, his heart to a pump, and his digestive system to a furnace consuming fuel.

Although many people do not consciously hold these views, they nevertheless tend to think of the living in terms of the machine. A large part of our time is occupied with mechanical contraptions, whether in travel, in communications, in labour-saving devices, or in forms of entertainment. Indeed there is hardly a human activity in which we do not rely on machines. Yet all that we receive by means of these brilliant inventions brings no true happiness. Until we can find once again the reality of man's being, our problems cannot be solved.

Rudolf Steiner showed that in our present epoch the loss of spiritual wisdom and the coming of materialism were necessary so that out of the void man could awaken his own powers to regain the knowledge he had lost. In this respect we can consider Parzival as a forerunner of our time.

In childhood he received no preparation for his future calling. When he went out into the world he had to find his way through trial and error, but in the wild forest where he grew up he had experienced wonder, which the Greeks considered to be the foundation of all knowledge. Through this wonder and through his delight in the world, revealed to him through his senses, he was gradually able to develop judgement. Today parents and teachers cannot give to the young people in their care guidance for all the contingencies they will have to meet. No one can know what situations the growing boy or girl is likely to experience, but it is important that during childhood we foster their innocent wonder and confidence in those who care for them.

Just as young people today have to find their way through conditions of uncertainty, Parzival had to live through the turmoil of the ninth century when the social order of the Middle Ages had not fully emerged. This is pictured in the general weakness of Arthur's court, where the King could no longer control the arrogance of knights such as Kay, Segramor and Ither of Gaheviess. It was a period without any strong central authority to prevent petty leaders from unauthorized violence. Orilus could seize Parzival's lands, Klamidé was able to besiege Kondwiramur's city in the hope of forcing her to marry him, and Meljanz could make unjustified war on Lippaut. The religious Order of the Grail, which should have brought a civilizing influence, was under eclipse.

Through his natural warmth of feeling Parzival was able to sympathize with those whom he saw suffer. He was moved to pity Siguné and was deeply affected when Kunnewaaré was struck for supporting him. His decision to champion Kondwiramur marked an important stage in his development for he here recognized a deeper bond than that of romantic love. He had also freed himself from the influences of the past as represented by Gurnemanz. At this point the impulse to seek his mother enabled him to be granted entry to the Grail Castle. But he had not attained the maturity to deal with the moral weakness of Anfortas.

The awakening of sympathetic understanding among young people today is of more importance than the teaching of currently accepted facts which will probably be superseded within a generation. Many of our apparently insoluble problems have been brought about by the complete lack of human relationships.

Like Parzival most young people today free themselves from parental control at an early age. It would be unthinkable to let their elders decide for them their profession, their friends or their marriage. But this early assertion of freedom leads to many mistakes for the faculty of sensing the true quality of their companions is rarely developed. Not all are able like Parzival to find their way in forming significant relationships. Social workers cannot deal with the countless problems of broken marriages, battered wives and babies, and general incompetence in dealing with daily pressures. Sympathy does not consist in allowing oneself to be swamped by others' sufferings, but in the understanding of the situation and in the strength to bring consolation.

The strengthening of Parzival's inner life came when he was able to free himself from the domination of the sense world and renounce his picture memories. Here Gawain was his helper. During the long separation from his wife and his exile from Arthur's court, he acquired steadfastness and self-reliance. Through his third meeting with Siguné and the contact with the old knight and his family, his heart was opened to accept the teaching of Trevrezent. Only when he had learned to acknowledge his guilt and meet death face to face in the encounter with Feirefis was he able to take over the burden of Anfortas's sin, as Trevrezent had taken over his.

We may now perhaps consider whether the qualities attained by Parzival are being developed among men today. We can find evidence both from the East and the West. There are two living writers, both Nobel prize-winners, who bring hope that out of the present disastrous conflicts new faculties are emerging.

At the end of his second volume of *Gulag Archipelago* Solzhenitzyn describes his personal experiences. After several years in the Russian labour camps he was overtaken by an apparently fatal illness. One night he was lying feverish and restless, when the camp doctor came to talk to him. He was Jewish but he described how he had come to accept Christianity and how ardently he had embraced the teachings of Christ. He ended by saying: 'Do you know that I have become convinced that no punishment comes to us in this life which is undeserved.'

Early in the morning the doctor was murdered—probably by some prisoner with a sordid grudge against him—so his words to Solzhenitsyn were his last on earth. The author felt them to be a legacy. He looked back over his own life and realized how self-centred he had been. As a brilliant young student he had taken it for granted that a successful future lay before him. He felt no gratitude for help given by others. He accepted the general conviction that all who got into trouble with the State were themselves to blame. Now he looked back and recognized that, without the shock which had brought him to suffer all the indignities of false accusations and inhuman treatment, he himself would have been as heartless as the tyrants who continued mercilessly to condemn millions of innocent people to imprisonment and death. He concluded that if all his own sufferings were considered inadequate, he could not murmur against such a judgment. He also saw that disaster could awaken new faculties. There were some in the camp who did not succumb, either to despair or to betraying their comrades for petty favours. For these, life came to have a new meaning. When they had lost everything except their own human dignity, they found the true values of freedom and friendship.

His pondering brought him to understand that one cannot overcome evil by fighting it. One may kill evil people, but then the evil spreads to others and the killers take the heritage of evil upon themselves. Evil can be overcome only by man's conquest of it within his own being. When he has mastered it within himself, then he develops the strength to have influence upon others.

We are presented with a different kind of evidence from the West, where the claim is made that human rights are recognized. Saul Bellow in his novel *Humboldt's Gift* gives a most negative picture of the American way of life. It appears from his account

67

that almost everyone is out for his own ends and in pursuit of them is prepared to deceive or betray his dearest friends without any pangs of conscience. Almost every institution is represented as corrupt. One can bear these descriptions only because they are narrated with so much caustic humour.

Charlie Citrine, the chief character in the story, after many highly successful years as a writer, met with a series of misfortunes. At this point in his career a friend introduced him to the teaching of Rufolf Steiner. Citrine felt that this was worth examining, and the book describes in some detail his studies and his following through of the meditations. Gradually he came to realize that here was a new way of life. It was possible to follow a path of active thinking which led to experiences of far greater value than worldly success. The more Citrine met with disaster in his outer life, the less it disturbed him, for he had found an inward source of hope and strength.

In his early life Citrine had very much admired an idealistic friend, Humboldt, and of whom everyone had expected a brilliant future. But Humboldt never fulfilled these hopes and had sunk into an obscurity of which his successful friends were ashamed. Later when Citrine himself was unfortunate he found that Humboldt had bequeathed to him a film script which had hitherto lain unused. To Citrine's astonishment this became a box office triumph. Since he had been through the experience of financial straits, he now knew how to use the money to help others.

Both these books describe the central character as receiving a legacy. There is here a recognition of the assistance given by those who have left the physical world. Moral impulses still live on after death. We also see represented two paths by which one can reach a higher level of consciousness and a deeper understanding of one's fellow men, the path of suffering as described by Solzhenitsyn, or of self-training as related by Bellow.

With Parzival these two paths led into one. Although in his outer actions he was always successful, he knew after his departure from the Grail Castle that, judged from a higher standpoint, he had failed, and this brought him deep suffering which culminated in the realization of his own guilt. However, at the same time he was disciplining himself—in his constant search for the Grail, in his faithfulness to his wife, and in his steadfast endeavour to put right the faults of his youth.

Parzival brought with him the strength of soul he had gained through a previous life. Rudolf Steiner revealed that Parzival was a reincarnation of the great Christian teacher Manes. The average man or woman of today has not this inborn power, but we have been given by Rudolf Steiner a path of training so that we can begin to develop the faculties which lead to a deeper understanding of man and of the world.

Our everyday thinking is conditioned by our sense impressions and by the opinions we receive through the modern media— books, newspapers, radio and television. These bind us firmly to the outer world. But Rudolf Steiner has shown that we can achieve a cognition that transcends that of our senses. Even through the simplest exercises in meditation as suggested in *Practical Training in Thinking*,[12] we can become aware of what lies behind outer forms. We then realize that all objects, whether man-made or manifestations of nature, come into being and disappear again, yet we can unite our thoughts with the processes of becoming and dying. We find that we can never experience the whole cycle by means of our senses, which only reveal images separated by time. But through our thinking we can unite what appears separate and bring it into relationship with the surrounding world. We then become aware that whatever man has made has been created through the activity of his intelligence. He has adapted what he finds in the world of nature and developed it to satisfy human needs or human tastes. Still more do the manifestations of nature, whether in forests or mountains, in the forms of crystals and the life cycles of plants and animals, appear as revelations of wisdom and beauty. For example, from the quite simple state of being of a seed more and more complex and lovely forms arise in leaf and blossom and fruit. Man too can transform his surroundings through the creations of true art.

In this way we can recognize our thinking as a living activity. We find that our thoughts grow and mature, and the ever-changing forms of nature illustrate for us the striving of the human being to unfold his higher powers. The one who can develop this faculty strongly enough becomes capable of receiving Imaginations such as those experienced by Parzival in the Grail Castle.

An illuminating description of this process is to be found in *The Evolution of the World and of Humanity*,[13] the series of lectures given in Penmaenmawr in August 1923. Rudolf Steiner here shows that Imaginations can bring great happiness but they cannot give us the power to understand others or to act rightly in practical life. Parzival's first experiences in the Grail Castle did not enable him to redeem Anfortas.

We need to reach a higher stage and the exercise for this requires a more strongly disciplined control. There is a danger that once we experience joy in our enlivened thinking we may give way to the pleasure of indulging in our imaginations. We then readily fall into illusions. As a safeguard against these a stern training is necessary. We have to learn to drive out all we have thought and pictured, and wait only in silent expectation. At this point one generally falls asleep or finds that unwanted thoughts and feelings keep straying into the emptied consciousness. Nevertheless, the effort itself can bring some result, for we have been renouncing that which has given us joy. We are now led to imagine ourselves withdrawing from the tumult of a noisy city into the silence of a deep wood where no sound can reach us. Then we should try to penetrate even further than silence into a boundless void. The one who can reach this stage learns to know that nothing can come into being without pain and endurance, and only he who deeply enters into this feeling can attain to Inspiration which gives the faculty to sense the being of others.

The third exercise demands a widening of our sympathies through the development of interest and concern for all aspects of life. This can come only when we learn to realize the part played in human progress by every living being or inanimate object: the flies that we destroy as germ-bearers are our most effective scavengers; poisonous plants are the sources of healing medicines; fierce animals can be brought to serve and be devoted to man.

It is more difficult to accept the part played by evil human beings. However, we have to recognize that for man to be free, out of his own choice to serve the good he has to have the chance of taking the opposite path. The presence of those who oppose and obstruct awakens consciousness. The first essential is to recognize the impulses of evil within ourselves, and then we can not only overcome the urge to punish and avenge but also learn to understand what powers have gripped hold of the evil-doers. The highest love is not a sentimental sympathy for the aberrations of others but a vision of what man is capable of becoming and an ability to aid him upon the path. The gift of being able to redeem through the right vision and the right deed is called by Rudolf Steiner 'Intuition'. This can be possible only through the help of the Christ.

Parzival developed through three stages from dullness, through doubt to blessedness, and this was a long and gradual process. Man today has to follow the same path. We are at a stage where our traditional spiritual wisdom has been entirely lost, but there lives hidden within each human being the longing to find again the sources of existence. This cannot now be achieved through blind acceptance of a faith which is taken on trust; it can be won only through questioning and strict self-training in the earnest endeavour to discover the truth.

There are signs today that a number of people are developing some stage of higher consciousness. Television programmes are given up to the discussion of supersensible experiences. Although not all of these can be taken seriously, the possibility of a wider range of perceptions than those dependent on our senses is viewed with tolerance.

There is a changed attitude to the world of nature. We have observed in the last few years the destructive effects of our reckless use of natural resources. The interest in preserving plant and animal life is now widespread. John Stewart Collis in *The Worm Forgives the Plough* describes labouring on a farm during the last war. His sensitive observations and ponderings on the seasons of the year, on the life-cycle of such plants as the potato or the couch-grass, and on the activities of the worm, are truly imaginative and one might consider that he had practised some of the exercises suggested by Rudolf Steiner.

There has also been a change in the view taken of those who are handicapped or incompetent. At the end of the last century there were well respected families who hid away mentally defective children and sent away the 'black sheep' of the family to some distant colony. Now there is great concern for all abnormal conditions whether of body or mind, and patients are helped as far

71

as possible to lead normal lives as accepted members of a social circle.

Many young people are drawn to help those in need of special care. Among the numerous examples of their work, *Bury Me in my Boots* by Sally Trench gives a moving account of her impulse to aid alcoholics and drug addicts. She was above all concerned with the hardened old meths drinkers and felt it important that they were not left to die alone.

There was lately a comment in the *Times* that the number of suicides in England has dropped during the last year, whereas in most Western countries it is on the increase. It was suggested that this was due to the devoted work of the Samaritans.[14] While politicians seem powerless and the industrial magnates have no solutions for our economic problems, we see that there are spheres in which individuals can be effective. New impulses for the future are not brought about by legislation or by military force; they can come only through the development of those powers which were first acquired as personal capacities by Parzival and are slowly appearing among human beings today.

When Trevrezent told the story of the first murder, Parzival became aware that he too, although not out of conscious malice, was guilty of the sin of Cain. The task of the Grail knights was to redeem the deed which had defiled the earth and sown hatred between man and man. The overcoming of evil is our most urgent task today and it cannot be lightly undertaken or easily accomplished, but then what seem the misfortunes of our present situation can become the spurs to greater effort.

In the opening lines of his poem Eschenbach describes his hero as 'a brave man slowly wise', and as a commentary on his gradual development it is perhaps fitting to quote here a verse composed by Rudolf Steiner:[15]

We are not granted
A rest on any step;
The active man
Must live and strive
From life to life,
As plants renew themselves
From spring to spring,
So man must rise
Through error to truth,
From fetters into freedom,
Through sickness and through death
To beauty, health and life.

THE INFLUENCE OF THE STARS AS ILLUSTRATED IN THE POEM OF *PARZIVAL*

E schenbach's poem contains references to the influence of the stars upon earthly events. In Book 9 he explains that his master Kyot had received the source of the story from a heathen, Flegetanis, who could tell how all the stars set and rose and how long each revolved before returning to its starting point once more. He knew how men's destinies were linked to the courses of the circling stars. With his own eyes he had read many secrets in the constellations and there he had learned of the Grail.

This implies that the course of Parzival's life was related to the movements of the stars, and, from time to time, in the poem we hear of the relationship of the planets to special events.

During the Egypto–Chaldean and the Greek epochs, it was accepted that man as a microcosm reflected within himself all that took place in the universe. The position of the sun in a particular sign of the zodiac at the time of conception was held to influence the character and course of life of the child about to be born, while the relationship of the planets bestowed certain capacities and shades of temperament. Rudolf Steiner has expressed in a verse for meditation the teaching in the Mystery Centre of Ephesus concerning the gifts of the planetary beings to man.

> Thou being born of Worlds and formed in Light,
> Strengthened by power of Sun and might of Moon,
> Thou art endowed with Mars' creative tones,
> And Mercury's fleet-footed rhythmic pulse,
> Jupiter's raying wisdom doth enlight thee,
> And Venus sheds her beauty-bearing Love,
> That Saturn's age-old Spirit-inwardness
> May hallow thee in realms of Space and Time.

This outlook was still taken for granted in the Middle Ages. In *The Divine Comedy* Dante describes the life after death of the souls who had attained Paradise. Each, according to his or her natural disposition, had an abiding place in one of the planetary spheres. For example, the lovers had their home in Venus; the warlike in Mars; the great teachers of religion in the Sun; and the contemplative in Saturn. All, however, when summoned, were united in the highest heaven around the throne of God.

It was held that during each period of life a particular planet dominated. During the first seven years, when the child was still strongly connected with the mother, the Moon had its ascendancy. From age 7 to 14, in the period of lively childish curiosity, Mercury held sway. Venus was influential in the years from age 14 to 21, when the first impulses of romantic love began to dawn. From 21 to 42, the human being entered fully into adult life and the Sun was then most powerful. The following seven years were under the leadership of Mars. Then came Jupiter, the representative of wise judgement. Finally from the age of 56 to 63 Saturn ruled over the years given up to contemplation and to memories. After this the human being brought all to harmony within himself.

In the case of great leaders or characters of genius, these stages could be passed through more rapidly or different capacities gained simultaneously. Parzival himself had imbibed all influences at an early age. When Kondrie appeared the second time she announced that the seven planets, whom she called by their Arabic names, confirmed Parzival's good fortune in being summoned to the Grail. This implies that he had received and harmonized the characteristics bestowed by all. We can trace through the course of his life their various influences. He was in the realm of the Moon when he lived with his mother in the forest of Soltane. The dominance of Mercury is apparent in the time of his youthful follies. When he was stirred by romantic love for Liasse, he was passing through the Venus period. From his conscious choice of Kondwiramur until his banishment from Arthur's court, he was a representative of the forces of the Sun. This is illustrated by the effect of his arrival on the knights of the Grail. 'It seemed to both old and young as though from him a new day shone.' Also, when he was led by Gawain into Arthur's court and his helmet was removed, it is said 'his face shone fair as though dewy roses had flown there'. After his banishment by Kondrie, he wandered alone, engaged in ceaseless combat under the guidance of Mars. From Trevrezent, when he received the teaching which enabled him to understand the course of his life, he attained the virtue of Jupiter. In his recognition of guilt and his renunciation of striving for the Grail, he was living with the forces of Saturn. There are many instances when we could say that some of these influences were apparent at an earlier stage. For instance, Mars was active in all his combats, and when he declined to remain with Gurnemanz he was already acquiring the power of judgement bestowed by Jupiter. But these qualities were not yet fully mastered. Only when Parzival was called to the Grail the second time had all been brought into balance.

When after their fierce conflict Parzival and his half-brother came to recognize each other, Feirefis declared, 'My mighty god Jupiter has warranted me this happiness.' In his general outlook and temperament Feirefis was very much under the influence of Mars, as can be seen from his ambition to win fame in war and from his eagerness on the way to the Grail Castle to attack the Templar Knights, but he was seeking wisdom. He realized Parzival's superiority, and said, 'Jupiter has bestowed his care upon you, you noble hero!'

We may consider that it was not only Jupiter but all the planets which had played a part in their conflict. The favourable outcome was not only owing to Fierefis's nobility in refusing to continue the fight with an unarmed opponent, but also to the impression Parzival had made upon him as a greater warrior than himself. They had been saved from the tragedy of a brother slaying a brother. Parzival, who had been guilty of the sin of Cain, was about to be accepted into the fellowship of those who were striving to make good the evil effects of Cain's deed. In his meeting with Fierefis he had now compensated for his earlier errors.

The wound of Anfortas was affected by the movements of the planets. Trevrezent told Parzival that the pain varied with the changes of the Moon, but the anguish was most acute when Saturn was at its zenith at the time of summer snow. Then the King became so cold that the poisoned spear had to be thrust into the wound to draw forth the frost. It is understandable that Saturn, the bringer of memory, should awake in Anfortas the fullest suffering on account of his sin.

During the last decades there has been a renewed interest in the influence of the stars on the world of nature and the life of man. The Greeks considered that no man could escape his fate. Today there is a different outlook. Certain events may be inevitable and much that happens is beyond our control, but man is free in his way of receiving what comes to him. Many may helplessly submit to misfortune, but the one who accepts his fate positively can learn from his experiences and bring about new situations. In the story of Parzival it is clear that, although the hero was called to the Grail service and his name was proclaimed in the stars, he himself had to develop his latent powers and earn the right to his position.

A COMPARISON OF ESCHENBACH'S
PARZIVAL WITH OTHER GRAIL ROMANCES

After the spread of Christianity among the Germanic tribes, the Church discouraged interest in the great pre-Christian epics, but from the eleventh century onwards, in France and later in Germany, the troubadours and minnesingers developed a new art in their popular romances. The earliest of these were the Chansons de Gestes, celebrating the heroic deeds of Charlemagne and Roland, or Dietrich of Bern. Then Celtic legends became popular, probably through the influence of Breton minstrels, and there appeared a whole series of Arthurian romances. Into these in the thirteenth century was woven the Grail theme.

If we accept the suggestion of many scholars that the concept of the Grail was a revival of the Celtic Imagination of the Cauldron of Plenty, we are failing to recognize the change of consciousness between pre-Christian and medieval times. The religious leaders of the Celts were well aware that our physical bodies are nourished and enlivened by spiritual powers, but the tellers of the Grail stories were inspired by a new impulse. They were concerned with the problem of sin and its destructive effect on the bodily organism of man, which had been degenerating since the loss of ancient spiritual wisdom. In pre-Christian times it was considered necessary in many tribes to expose children who were born deformed and to condemn to death any whose conduct threatened the tribal law, but through Christianity there had been fostered the impulse to heal and redeem. Owing to the increasing dogmatism of the Church, this could not be openly proclaimed, but those who possessed supersensible knowledge were able to present this teaching in the form of imaginative pictures. These appeared in the Grail stories.

In medieval romances the Grail is presented in many different forms, but it has always the quality of receiving and bestowing spiritual grace and wisdom. It can be described as a stone, a cup, a chalice, or the vessel used at the Last Supper. The moon can appear as a Grail, not only because the crescent before Easter can be seen as a chalice, but also because it receives light and power from the sun and passes them on to the earth to awaken life processes in plant, animal and man. The human body can also be regarded as a vessel which the soul and spirit inhabit in order to transform the earth. In this sense the most noble expression of the Grail is the body of Jesus of Nazareth which became the bearer of the Christ.

When Eschenbach describes the Grail as a stone, he relates it to the most beautiful jewel in Lucifer's crown which was redeemed and guarded by the Templar Knights to become the foundation of a new spiritual wisdom. Christ spoke of himself as 'the stone which the builders rejected' which then became 'the head of the corner'. In the Apocalypse the new Jerusalem is likened to 'a stone most precious, even like a jasper stone, clear as crystal'.

When Eschenbach describes the Grail as 'a thing', this word is not used in the trivial sense which is taken for granted today. We can compare the expression with Gabriel's words to Mary in St Luke's Gospel, 'that holy thing which shall be born of thee shall be called the Son of God'.

With later Grail romances, such as the Lancelot sequence translated by Malory, the Grail is the chalice of the Last Supper in which Joseph of Arimathaea gathered the blood flowing from the Saviour's side as He hung upon the cross.

We need to be able to judge which of the romances offer true Imaginations and which present confused pictures where the teller is not aware of their real meaning. Unlike Homer many of the poets of the Middle Ages did not receive inspiration from a divine Muse, but drew their subject matter from any available source that provided a good story. During the long winter evenings the inmates of the baronial castles had need of entertainment, so they appreciated endless episodes describing the adventures of favourite knights. Scenes of magic were all the more fascinating when they could not be explained. Then, to avoid the danger of condemnation by the Church, the teller would introduce passages of moral teaching. Some of the later Grail stories are crowded with Biblical allusions or references to holy relics, which do not add in any way to the development of the story.

Apart from Eschenbach's poem there are four romances connected with Parzival which are obtainable in English. The story of Peredur, translated from the Welsh of the *Mabinogion* by Lady Guest, is thought to be the earliest. The adventures of the young Peredur, from his childhood in the forest until his appearance at Arthur's court and the slaying of the Red Knight, closely resemble those of Eschenbach's hero. After this the adventures become confused. Peredur meets with a lame old man, whose attendants are fishing, and learns from him not to ask questions. He comes to a castle where two youths bear into the hall a mighty spear, dripping with blood. They are followed by two maidens carrying a salver containing the bloodstained head of a man. There is no mention of a Grail. There follow a great number of disconnected adventures in the course of which a beautiful woman, who turns out to be an empress, gives him a stone of invisibility. An ugly creature resembling Kondrie drives Peredur from Arthur's court because he failed to ask the question which would have healed the lame man. At the end we learn that the laming of the old man and the slaying of the one whose head was carried in the salver were the deeds of the sorceresses of Gloucester, whom Peredur with Arthur's help finally destroys.

The confusion of this story seems to show that the teller had heard a version of the Grail legend and gathered incidents from it without any understanding of the central theme. Some of the episodes are told with a primitive vigour which gives them a certain appeal, but this is hardly a Grail romance.

The High History of the Holy Grail, translated from the French by Sebastian Evans, has as its central theme the quest for the Grail by Perceval, Gawain and Lancelot. In spite of the many irrelevant adventures, there is some recognition of the characters of the different knights and the reasons for their failure or success.

The first episode shows that the teller no longer understood the relationship of the dream world with that of everyday life. A squire, who is due to accompany King Arthur on a quest, dreams that he oversleeps and has to gallop in haste after his master. He comes to a lonely chapel where he yields to the temptation to steal a golden candlestick. He is attacked and sorely wounded. He wakes up to find that the whole incident was a dream, but the candlestick is by his side and he is mortally wounded.

Early in the story we learn that the Fisher King is languishing because Perceval, on visiting the Grail Castle, did not ask whom the Grail served. Through his failure the maiden bearing the Grail has become bald and carries her right arm in a sling.

Gawain is eager to take on the question but is not allowed to enter the Grail Castle unless he brings with him the sword which beheaded John the Baptist. When he has succeeded in this task and returns, he is reminded by everyone he meets to ask the question which will restore the Fisher King. But when beholding the Grail procession, he is so swept away by his feelings of devotion and bliss that he forgets everything.

The Grail ritual is different from the one described by Eschenbach. One maiden holds a lance which drips blood while a second gathers the drops into the Grail. To Gawain the vessel appears as a chalice, and he beholds two angels carrying candlesticks of gold, while in the midst of the Grail shines the figure of a child. The narrator is bringing his account nearer to the celebration of the communion than does Eschenbach.

After Gawain's failure Lancelot undertakes the task. On his way to the castle he meets with a hermit to whom he confesses his sins. The hermit implores him to renounce his unlawful love for the Queen. Lancelot replies, 'This sin will I reveal to you of my lips, but of my heart may I never repent me thereof.' He is willing to do penance but not to change. When he comes to the castle, the mystery of the Grail is not revealed to him for he loves the Queen more than he loves the Grail.

When at last Perceval returns, he finds that the lord of the Castle Mortal has conquered the realm of the Fisher King, who is now dead. With the blessing of a company of hermits and the help of two magical beasts, a white mule and a white lion, Perceval is able to win back the kingdom. After most of his men have been slaughtered, the lord of Castle Mortal kills himself, and when the last of the enemies has been driven out, the Grail, which has temporarily withdrawn, reappears. The importance of asking the question is never made clear, but Perceval's failure and the Fisher King's languishing are explained by the hermit as the will of God.

The story does not end here. The three chief knights still

continue to have many aimless adventures which offer opportunities for moral teaching. At last Perceval is summoned on board a ship bearing a white sail with a red cross which bears him away into the unknown. Though certain of the episodes are told with great charm, the work as a whole is a notable example of the confusion of themes in many of the later medieval romances.

The Romance of Perceval in Prose, translated by Dell Skeels, still more fully illustrates the story-teller's delight in weaving well-known incidents around his chosen hero, without any consideration for a central theme. The beginning and the end of the tale are concerned with King Arthur, and the narrator has no conception of the difference between the Arthurian and the Grail cults. In the opening chapter Merlin tells Arthur the history of how our Lord appeared to Joseph of Arimathaea in prison and gave him the chalice containing His blood. This was passed down to members of Joseph's family. However, the present King Bron has fallen into a great sickness. He cannot die until a knight of the Round Table finds his way to the castle and asks whom the Grail serves.

In the next chapter we meet Perceval who, in obedience to his father's dying wish, rides to the court of King Arthur, where he is kindly received and in due course becomes a knight. He falls in love with Gawain's sister and, when fighting in her honour, surpasses all other knights including Sir Lancelot. The 12 chief knights occupy the 12 seats at the Round Table, but there is a vacant thirteenth reserved for the best knight in the world. In spite of Arthur's refusal, Perceval claims the right to this place. As soon as he sits down, the stone seat, with a violent crack, splits in two. Then a voice proclaims that never will the stone be reunited or the Fisher King restored until the best knight in the world finds the castle and asks whom the Grail serves. Many knights, including Perceval, set out in quest.

In the meantime, unknown to Perceval his mother has died of grief. However, he does not, as related by Eschenbach, go in search of her. Later, when meeting with his sister who tells him of her death, he visits his hermit uncle to confess his fault.

Perceval has many adventures and encounters with dark, magical forces, but these have little connection with the main theme except to make clear that he is the best knight in the world. When at last he comes to the Grail Castle, although he has been

82

told about the importance of the question, he does not ask because his mother has taught him that he should not talk too much. There is no mention of his passing a disturbed night or of his being thrown out of the castle, but after leaving it he meets a weeping maiden who reproaches him for his failure. She does not appear again.

When he cannot find his way back to the castle, Perceval is seized with a fit of madness—an affliction often attributed to Lancelot. He is brought to his senses when he meets a party of pilgrims who reproach him for wearing armour on a holy day. He finds his way to his hermit uncle but receives no help except his blessing. After further adventures, however, he meets the magician Merlin who tells him that he has failed to find the Grail Castle because he has not been faithful to a vow he made when setting out on the quest. He swore at that time that, until he succeeded, he would not sleep more than one night in any place. Perceval replies that he has not lately given thought to this. Merlin comments, 'Then you may be the more easily forgiven.' He assures Perceval that he will in due course come to his destination.

When Perceval returns to the castle and asks whom the Grail serves, the King is restored. The voice of the Holy Ghost then commands that Bron should appoint Perceval as his successor and teach him the sacred words which our Lord taught to Joseph in prison when he gave the chalice into his keeping. After three days Bron departs from this life and Perceval has a vision of David and many angels waiting to receive his soul.

At the moment of the healing of the Fisher King, the stone seat at the Round Table is reunited and the story returns to King Arthur. We hear of the last fight and the end of the Order of the Round Table. However, it is told that Arthur does not die but withdraws to the Isle of Avalon whence he will return when his country is in need.

There is a mood of unreality in the whole story and it completely lacks the powerful human appeal of Eschenbach's *Parzival*. Very few places or characters are clearly described and the incidents seem to take place in a world of fantasy. At the end we hear that Merlin has observed everything and his fellow magician Blayse has kept the records so that nothing may be forgotten. This adds to the impression that the tale belongs to the realm of magic.

Malory's version of the Grail story is the most widely known in

England. The *Morte Darthur* is a translation of several French works, and, as most of the episodes are concerned with Arthur and his circle, many people are confused as to the relationship of the Arthurian order and the Grail. However, when a number of his knights set out to seek for the Grail, Arthur is deeply grieved and reproaches Gawain and Lancelot for deserting him and destroying the Fellowship of the Round Table. This clearly indicates the difference between the two impulses. In the stories adapted by Malory, Lancelot had become the leading hero. He appears in many different adventures but one theme is common to all and that is his unlawful love for Queen Guinevere. On this account he could not be presented as the one to attain the Grail. Nevertheless, story-tellers felt the need to link their most popular hero with his ideal, and so he was made to appear as the father of the one who would become the Grail King. In the version followed by Malory, the way in which this is brought about may not seem justified. It is told how in the Grail circle it was known that Lancelot, according to destiny, was the one appointed to marry the daughter of its Guardian, King Pelles, but, owing to his love for Guinevere, he would never consider accepting this position. A deception was then practised upon him. He was led to Pelles's daughter Elaine and cast under a spell so that he imagined he was lying with the Queen. From this union was born Galahad of whom it was foretold that he should achieve the Grail. We might well consider such a ruse unworthy of a spiritual leader, but it is possible to view this episode in a different light. Lancelot was 'human, all too human', and therefore unfitted to serve the Grail, but, through trials and sufferings, like the majority of mankind, he was willy-nilly acquiring nobler qualities. Galahad can be regarded as an Imagination of what Lancelot could become in the distant future. He is presented not as a human being but as an angelic being, protected from all temptation and untouched by any sin. His deeds appear in the light of miracles. If we accept the view that, after many incarnations, the human being can free himself from the fetters of the sense world and become the embodiment of his spiritual ideals, we can think of Galahad as a reflection of Lancelot's higher being.

In the *Morte Darthur*, the Grail was not guarded by a community which through its grace was able to serve the outer world. It bestowed an individual mystical ecstasy, granted only to those who were free of all human desires, though in certain cases the blessing might be received through the mediation of another, as is later illustrated in the cases of Sir Perceval and Sir Bors. At Lancelot's first meeting with Pelles he was granted this vision, perhaps as a summons to awake to his true destiny and renounce the Queen. It is told that, as he and the Guardian sat together, a dove came in at the window, bearing a little censer of gold, whereupon they were provided with all the nourishment they required. Then a maiden entered carrying a vessel of gold before which King Pelles knelt and said his prayers. Lancelot asked, 'What may this mean?' 'This,' said the King, 'is the holy Sangreal, and, when this thing goeth about, the Round Table shall be broken.' However, after his union with Elaine, Lancelot was no longer granted such an experience.

When Galahad became its Guardian, the Grail disappeared from the West, which had sunk too far into materialism; so he was guided to the holy city of Sarras. At this time it was widely believed that only in the East, where Christ had lived and suffered, could one truly be united with His impulse. Perceval appears only as a minor participant, experiencing the Mystery under Galahad's leadership.

Galahad prayed that he might be permitted to leave this earthly life and, after he had served for a year as King in Sarras, his prayer was granted. He was received into the spiritual world and the spear and the lance were taken with him to be seen no more on earth.

The healing of the sick King plays a little part in the story. Pelles had seized a sword which he was not worthy to wield and had been wounded through both thighs. After attaining the leadership of the Grail, Galahad restored him to health, but neither Pelles nor his son was any longer connected with its service.

In the *Morte Darthur* many of the episodes connected with the Grail are beautifully told and deeply moving, so that readers often find themselves in an enchanted world where they are willing to be led from one adventure to another without feeling the need to understand their meaning. But for those who look for a well constructed development, the endless series of disconnected

85

incidents, visions and dreams, which serve to illustrate religious teaching, become somewhat wearisome.

In comparing Eschenbach's poem with the three narratives described above, we can marvel at its consistency. He preserves a fine balance between descriptions of the supersensible and of the earthly realms, for he reveals on the one hand the deepest strivings of the human soul, yet on the other he recognizes the demands and duties of everyday life. The story is developed step by step, each incident playing a necessary part and each single detail having its significance. The hero's character unfolds in its steady progress from dullness through doubt to blessedness, and the attainment of the Grail leads not to an escape from earthly responsibilities but to their fulfilment. The whole work is remarkably free from any dogmatic teaching. Whatever he wished to impress upon his audience was given through imaginative pictures or through incidents in the story. As the poem appeared in the form of a romance, Wolfram was able to give free expression to his imagination without danger of being accused of heresy. Although he did not actually contradict the teaching of the Catholic Church, like Dante he was able to indicate through a work of art deeper esoteric truths. The Grail ritual took place in a castle not in a church, and was administered by a woman and not a priest. Trevrezent, who absolved Parzival, had never been ordained, and Parzival's election as Grail King received no sanction from any established religious order. At the beginning of the thirteenth century it was still possible for a certain freedom of thought to flourish without being suppressed, and the poem was widely known and appreciated. It was with the advent of Protestantism that the medieval romances fell into disfavour, but in times of need great works of art reappear to give their inspiration to a new age.

NOTES AND REFERENCES

1 Wolfram von Eschenbach, *Parzival, a Knightly Epic*, trans. Jessie L. Weston (London: David Nutt, 1894).

2 Wolfram von Eschenbach, *Parzival, A Romance of the Middle Ages*, trans. Helen Mustard and Charles Passage (New York: Vintage Books, 1961). (Editor's note: see also *Parzival*, trans. A.T. Hatto (Penguin Classics, 1980.)

3 *The Mabinogion*, trans. Lady Charlotte Guest (Dent, Everyman edition).

4 (Tr) Brian Stone, *Sir Gawain and the Green Knight* (Penguin Classics).

5 Rudolf Steiner, *Cosmic Christianity*, six lectures given in England, 1924 (London: Anthroposophical Publishing Co., 1953). Also published as Vol. VIII of *Karmic Relationships* (Rudolf Steiner Press, 1975).

6 A version of the Tristan and Isolde legend, collected from the best French sources, can be recommended: Joseph Bédier, *The Romance of Tristan and Iseult*, trans. Hilaire Belloc (Allen & Unwin).

7 Albert Steffen, *The Death Experience of Manes* (New York: Folder Editions).

8 Zoe Oldenbourg, *Massacre at Montségur*, trans. Peter Green (Weidenfeld and Nicholson).

9 Emile Mâle, *The Gothic Image, The Religious Art in France of the Thirteenth Century*, trans. Dora Nussey (London and New York: Harper & Row, Icon edition).

10 W.J. Stein, *Die Geschichte des Neunte Jahrhunderts im Lichte des Heiligen Grals* (Stuttgart: Mellinger Verlag). (Editor's note: now available as *The Ninth Century*, trans. revised by John M. Wood, Temple Lodge Press, 1991.)

11 Rudolf Steiner, *Knowledge of the Higher Worlds—How is it Achieved?*, revised trans. by D.S. Osmond and C. Davy (Rudolf Steiner Press, 1976).

12 Rudolf Steiner, *Practical Training in Thinking*, Trans. George Adams (Rudolf Steiner Press, 1969).

13 Rudolf Steiner, Penmaenmawr lectures, 1923, published as *The*

Evolution of Consciousness, trans. V.E. Watkin and C. Davy (Rudolf Steiner Press, 1966).

14 Chad Varah, *The Samaritans* (Constable). The opening sentences of the Preface: 'The Samaritans are several thousand men and women who dedicate a generous part of their leisure time to the prevention of suicide. Theirs are the quiet unhurried voices which, at any hour of the day or night, any day of the year, answer one of over fifty emergency telephones with the words, "Samaritans—can I help you?"'

15 Verse by Rudolf Steiner in commemoration of the German romantic poet Holderlin.